# THE COMPLETE
# GERRY ANDERSON
# EPISODE GUIDE

# OTHER GERRY ANDERSON BOOKS AVAILABLE

**THUNDERBIRDS novels**

1. Thunderbirds by John Theydon
Coming soon:
2. Calling Thunderbirds by
John Theydon

**CAPTAIN SCARLET novels**

1. Captain Scarlet and the Mysterons by
John Theydon
Coming soon:
2.Captain Scarlet and the Silent Saboteur
by John Theydon

# OTHER FILM AND TV BOOKS AVAILABLE

Doctor Who: The Scripts Books 1-4
Don't Panic: The Hitchhiker's Guide to
the Galaxy Companion
Fantastic Television
Giger's Alien
Mr Scott's Guide to the Enterprise
Ray Harryhausen's Film Fantasy
Scrapbook
The Best of Science Fiction Television
The Man from U.N.C.L.E. Book
The Official Batman Batbook
The Star Trek Compendium
The Star Trek Interview Book
The Worlds of the Federation

# THE COMPLETE

BY
ADAM
PIRANI

# GERRY ANDERSON

Titan
BOOKS

# EPISODE GUIDE

THE COMPLETE GERRY ANDERSON
EPISODE GUIDE

ISBN 1 85286 216 5

Published by
Titan Books Limited
58 St Giles High Street
London WC2H 8LH

First edition November 1989
10 9 8 7 6 5 4 3 2 1

Printed and bound by Maclehose &
Partners, Railway Triangle, Walton
Road, Portsmouth, England.

In 1956 an old friend of mine, Arthur Provis, agreed to join me in a venture to make our own films.

We operated as a partnership to begin with and for months we struggled along, slowly but surely heading towards bankruptcy.

At the eleventh hour we were asked to make a puppet series called *The Adventures of Twizzle* by the author, Roberta Leigh. There were to be fifty two fifteen-minute episodes and if we were to clinch the deal - which we needed desperately - we would have to sign a contract and to sign that contract we needed to form a limited company straight away.

We wanted to be sure of getting a name for the new company approved quickly, so we submitted no less than thirty four names to the registrar. All were turned down because they were all in use.

In desperation we submitted the name A.P. Films (Anderson and Provis). The registrar approved it - surprise, surprise, there was no other A.P. Films registered.

Of course, we were only going to use the name temporarily . . . but before long we had printed our notepaper and business cards and the name was in the telephone directory and becoming known in the industry. I recall that Arthur and I used to joke about it - he insisted that A.P. stood for Arthur Provis whilst I claimed that it stood for Anderson Productions.

In fact it was many years before we changed this 'temporary' name, and when we did it was changed to . . . Century 21.

## FOREWORD

Little did I know at the time that we were starting a production line that was to become legendary. We produced hundreds of programmes that were shown around the world, dubbed or subtitled into every major language. Every three years there was a new audience of children and so the shows were repeated and repeated. The merchandising, music and publishing were huge, but, perhaps most importantly for me, we led the way to today's big special effects movies.

The years have rolled by and now I can look back on a whole world filled with characters, cities and machines that have been created for all the shows for which I was responsible.

Titan Books have now meticulously researched my work to date and compiled this definitive episode guide. Not only does it cover all the shows I have made that have been transmitted but also one or two that didn't quite make it. It contains a wealth of photographs, together with cast and crew lists. If you are interested in my little worlds, then I am sure you will be interested to read this guide.

I should like to thank all those who have contributed to this work and in particular Mark Cox, Louise Griffiths, Rian Hughes, Bob Kelly, Henry Scott-Irvine and last, but certainly not least, Katy Wild.

Titan Books are also reprinting the paperbacks produced over the years and based on my shows. If you missed them, you'll now have a chance to catch up and if you didn't, you can take a trip down memory lane.

And talking of memories, this guide has triggered many for me - so much so that I have at last decided to start work on my biography. The publishers have been asking me to write it for many years.

Who are the publishers ?  Why, Titan Books - who else ?

Gerry Anderson

The following Anderson series are
available on video from Channel 5:

*STINGRAY*

*THUNDERBIRDS*

*CAPTAIN SCARLET*

*JOE 90*

*UFO*

*TERRAHAWKS*

*DICK SPANNER*

FANDERSON is a club for everyone
who enjoys the work of Gerry Anderson.
Send an SAE for full details to:
FANDERSON, 147 Francis Rd, London
E10 6NT.

## STAND BY FOR ACTION !

For over thirty years, the imaginative and innovative work of Gerry Anderson has been providing exciting entertainment for millions of television viewers. From his early days, with such traditional children's puppet shows as *The Adventures of Twizzle*, through the classic Supermarionation series: *Stingray*, *Thunderbirds*, *Captain Scarlet* and *Joe 90*, and into the live-action science fiction programmes, *UFO* and *Space 1999*, the breadth and individuality of his vision have stamped all of his work with a unique 'Anderson' quality.

This quality has made his shows, whether they feature puppets or live actors, studio sets or locations, instantly identifiable as Anderson productions. The familiar mixture of engaging heroes, evil villains, amazing craft and innovative special effects has become part of popular consciousness. It has had many imitators but no-one who has captured that unique 'Anderson' style.

It is this wonderful style and the scope of his phenomenal creativity that we have tried to capture in this book by providing, for the first time in collected form, an episode guide to every television series created by Gerry Anderson, in chronological order. Commencing with *Twizzle* and ending with *Dick Spanner*, each series has its own section, explaining the basic premise of the series and its location; the key characters and craft; story synopses of each episode in the series; and a short list of the principal credits.

## INTRODUCTION

Throughout we have tried to include as many black and white photographs as possible, and there is a special colour photograph section at the end of the book which provides a montage of some of the more memorable images from all the shows. In some instances, there has been very little undamaged photographic material to choose from and we hope the rarity of the stills used in such cases compensates for their slightly inferior quality.

We hope we have achieved the right balance, making the book as appealing to the armchair browser as it is to the committed fan. We are always happy to receive comments or suggestions for improvements for inclusion in future editions.

A work such as this is a mammoth task and many people must be thanked for their help along the way: Mary & Gerry Anderson, Doug Mead and Peter Harrington at ITC, Henry Scott-Irvine for picture research; David Nightingale and S.I.G. magazine; Richard Holliss at Forbidden Planet; Kim Hawson at Channel 5; Steve Kyte; Philip Rae of Polly Products; Chris Leach for help on *Four Feather Falls*; Peter Halsey for help on *The Adventures of Twizzle* and *Torchy the Battery Boy*; Brendan Sheehan for the *Supercar* and *Fireball XL5* episode synopses, which originally appeared in S.I.G.; and Ralph Titterton for help on *The Secret Service*.

*Dedicated to*
**GERRY ANDERSON**
*in recognition and appreciation of his
work in television and with thanks for
his unfailing support and belief in
this book.*

1957

Twizzle is a little boy doll who runs away from a toyshop. He befriends Footso, a black and white cat with enormous paws. Together they build a haven for stray toys called Stray Town. Here toys can live in safety apart from the children who mistreat them.

### Characters

TWIZZLE - the boy doll with blue trousers and a green wool cap. He has bright red hair and a round, shiny face. He can 'twizzle' himself as tall as a lamp-post and can 'twizzle' his arms and legs so that he can reach anything he wants.

FOOTSO - the black and white cat with enormous paws.

CHAWKY - the white-faced golliwog

JIFFY THE BROOMSTICK MAN

POLLY MOPPET

CANDY FLOSS - the mamma doll that can't say 'mamma'

BOUNCY - the ball who's lost his bounce.

## 1. TWIZZLE AND FOOTSO

Twizzle runs away from the toyshop and meets the cat, Footso.

## 2. TWIZZLE AND FOOTSO GET CAUGHT

Twizzle and Footso are forced to work for a crafty old man.

## 3. TWIZZLE SAVES THE DOLL

Twizzle saves a doll from a doll's house fire.

## 4. THE BREAKDOWN VAN

Twizzle swops his racing car for a breakdown van.

## 5. FOOTSO IS STOLEN

Footso is stolen by an old woman.

## 6. TWIZZLE AND THE GOLLIWOG

Twizzle and the Golliwog go skating and fall in the lake.

## 7. JIFFY AND CHAWKY QUARREL

Jiffy, the Broomstick Man, and Chawky quarrel.

## 8. FOOTSO DISAPPEARS

Footso tries to steal some fish and gets into trouble.

## 9. TWIZZLE AND THE BROKEN-DOWN TOY

Twizzle finds a mamma doll who can't say "Mamma".

## 10. TWIZZLE BUILDS STRAY TOWN

Twizzle builds a log cabin town where stray toys can live.

## 11. A FLAG FOR STRAY TOWN

Candy Floss makes a flag for Stray Town.

## 12. JIFFY'S NEW HOUSE

Twizzle builds Jiffy a new log cabin.

## 13. TWIZZLE AND FOOTSO GO FRUIT PICKING

Twizzle and Footso have a picnic and Footso swallows a bee.

## 14. TWIZZLE HAS SOME FUN

Footso eats Twizzle's lunch and Twizzle plays a trick on him.

## 15. TWIZZLE AND CANDY FLOSS OPEN A CAKE SHOP

Candy Floss makes some toffee and Chawky falls in the mixture.

**16. TWIZZLE SAVES THE BROKEN-DOWN TOYS**
Twizzle saves broken-down toys and takes them back to Stray Town.

**17. TWIZZLE GETS LOST**
Twizzle gets lost in Tweedle Town.

**18. JIFFY OPENS A BARBER SHOP**
Jiffy opens a shop to earn money to buy acorns.

**19. ANOTHER RACING CAR**
Twizzle borrows a racing car.

**20. TWIZZLE AND HIS FRIENDS GO TO THE CIRCUS**
Twizzle and his friends go to the circus.

**21. THE TOYS GO TO SCHOOL**
Twizzle becomes a teacher as the toys cannot read and write.

**22. BOUNCY THE BALL**
Bouncy the non-bouncing ball objects to being kicked around.

**23. JACK-IN-THE-BOX**
Twizzle becomes jealous of Jack-in-the-Box.

**24. TWIZZLE CATCHES COLD**
Twizzle is in bed with a cold.

**25. THE NAUGHTY GIRL**
Twizzle rescues a doll locked in a toy cupboard.

**26. JIFFY'S NEW TWIGS**
The toys go in search of new twigs to replace Jiffy's worn-out ones.

**OTHER TWIZZLE EPISODES (NOT WITH GERRY ANDERSON)**

27. TWIZZLE AND THE SNOWMAN

28. TWIZZLE AND THE THIN TEDDY BEAR

29. THE LAZY BROOMSTICK MAN

30. TWIZZLE AND POLLY MOPPET

31. FOOTSO AND THE MAGIC SEEDS

32. JIFFY AND POLLY MOPPET QUARREL

33. FOOTSO GETS A NEW TAIL

34. TWIZZLE IS NAUGHTY

35. TWIZZLE IS STOLEN

36. CHAWKY GETS A PRESENT

37. TWIZZLE AND THE TOY INSPECTOR

38. TWIZZLE AND THE NAUGHTY BREAKDOWN VAN

39. ORANGE AND BANANA TREE

40. JIFFY'S BIRTHDAY

41. POLLY MOPPET DISAPPEARS

42. NAUGHTY POLLY MOPPET

43. FOOTSO AND THE NAUGHTY GIRL

44. STRAY TOWN THIEF

45. TWIZZLE PAPERS THE CABIN

46. TWIZZLE AND FOOTSO GO CAMPING

47. TWIZZLE GOES TO THE SEASIDE

48. TWIZZLE GOES TO THE FAIR

49. TWIZZLE GOES FISHING

50. TWIZZLE GOES TO THE ZOO

51. CANDY FLOSS'S BIRTHDAY

52. FOOTSO HAS TOOTHACHE

**Principal credits**
52 fifteen minute episodes
Black and white
An AP Films Production for associated Rediffusion Network
Created and written by : Roberta Leigh
Directed by : Gerry Anderson (first 26 only)
Set Designer : Reg Hill
Puppetry Supervisor : Joy Laurey
Voice of Twizzle : Denise Bryer

1960

Torchy is a wind-up clockwork toy who, helped by Mr Bumbledrop, has beeen sent by rocket to Topsy Turvy Land - a land where mistreated or neglected toys from Earth can walk and talk as if they are human.

The ruler of Topsy Turvy Land is King Dithers who lives in the Orange Peel Palace. Torchy lives in Frutown with his toy friends, except when he returns to Earth on one of his trips. Only Torchy and Pom-Pom, the toy poodle, can return to Earth as they are clockwork, moving toys; other toys would revert to their usual, unmoving form.

### Characters

TORCHY THE BATTERY BOY -
the clockwork toy with a battery-
powered lamp on his helmet.
POM-POM -
the clockwork French poodle
FLOPSY - the rag doll
PILLIWIG - the toy clown
SPARKY - the baby dragon
SQUISH - the space boy
PONGO - the rag doll pirate
KING DITHERS -
ruler of Topsy Turvy Land
BOSSY BOOTS - the Earth girl

### 1. POM-POM AND THE TOYS

Introduces Torchy, the Battery Boy, and his friend Pom-Pom the poodle.

### 2. TOPSY TURVY LAND

Torchy meets Pom-Pom again in Topsy Turvy Land where toys can talk.

### 3. TORCHY AND SQUISH

Torchy is worried in case his battery runs down and he meets Squish.

### 4. THE BUILDING OF FRUTOWN

Pilliwig the clown helps Torchy and his friends build some unusual houses.

### 5. TORCHY AND THE BROKEN RACKET

Torchy and Squish meet the Ting-a-Ling Bird.

### 6. KING DITHERS

Torchy's search for cardboard takes him to Orange Peel Palace and he meets King Dithers.

### 7. TORCHY GOES BACK TO EARTH

Pom-Pom to the rescue as Torchy's battery is too low to return him to Earth.

### 8. BOSSY BOOTS GOES TO TOPSY TURVY LAND

Torchy meets Bossy Boots, a little girl who is rude to grown ups.

### 9. BOSSY BOOTS IS TAUGHT A LESSON

Flopsy tries to curb Bossy Boots' bad behaviour.

### 10. A BELL FOR THE PENNY FARTHING

King Dithers gives Torchy a penny farthing bicycle.

### 11. A TRICK ON POM-POM

Torchy and Flopsy decide to teach Pom-Pom a lesson.

### 12. TORCHY IS STOLEN

Mrs Meanymouth takes Torchy home and he has to be rescued.

### 13. KING DITHERS LOSES HIS CROWN

Torchy and King Dithers search for the King's lost crown.

### 14. PILLIWIG GETS A PRESENT

Torchy and Flopsy find someone to laugh at Pilliwig's jokes.

### 15. BAD BOY BOGEY

Torchy and Daffy give lessons in good manners.

### 16. TORCHY AND THE STRANGE ANIMAL

Torchy and Pom-Pom make friends with a baby dragon.

### 17. BOSSY BOOTS FORGETS TO BE GOOD

Torchy helps the hungry money box, Clinker, to find a good dinner.

### 18. THE HUNGRY MONEY BOX

Pongo the Pirate steals Clinker's breakfast and Torchy explores a gold mine.

### 19. THE NAUGHTY TWINS

Torchy has trouble with the twins, Bobby and Babs, and takes them to Topsy Turvy Land for a lesson.

### 20. THE TWINS LEARN A LESSON

The naughty twins are taught a lesson by the Pollikan Bird.

### 21. KING DITHERS GOES DOWN TO EARTH

King Dithers sets out for Earth but lands on the Moon by mistake.

### 22. TORCHY IS SAVED AT LAST

Bossy Boots is naughty again and Torchy gets his rocket back.

### 23. TORCHY AND THE MAN IN THE MOON

Torchy takes Mr Bumbledrop to the Moon.

### 24. BOGEY AND THE STATUES

Torchy has trouble with Bogey and has to nurse the ill Mr Bumbledrop.

### 25. THE MOON FALLS ASLEEP

Torchy and the toys find the Moon has stopped shining and Torchy investigates.

### 26. TORCHY'S BIRTHDAY

Torchy's birthday cake contains a special surprise.

**Principle Credits**
26 fifteen minute episodes
Black and white
An AP Films Production for
Associated Rediffusion Network
Created and Written by :
Roberta Leigh
Directed by : Gerry Anderson
Art Director : Reg Hill
Puppetry Supervisor :
Christine Glenville

1960

# FOUR FEATHER FALLS

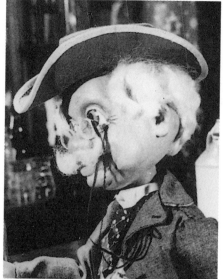

## Characters

TEX TUCKER - sheriff of Four Feather Falls
DUSTY - the sheriff's dog
ROCKY - the sheriff's horse
MA JONES -
the general store proprietor
MARVIN JACKSON -
the bank manager
DAN MORSE - the telegraphist
DOC HAGGETY - the doctor
SLIM JIM - owner and bartender of the
Denison saloon
LITTLE JAKE - a small boy
TWINK - Little Jake's grandpa
RED SCALP - the renegade Indian chief
PEDRO AND FERNANDO -
the Mexican bandits

## Premise

The action is set in Four Feather Falls, Kansas, a long time ago. The sheriff, Tex Tucker, keeps order with the help of his dog, Dusty, and his horse, Rocky. As a reward for fuinding and saving an Indian boy, Tex was given four magic feathers - two give Dusty and Rocky the power of speech, and two enable Tex's guns to swivel and fire automatically in times of danger.

### 1. HOW IT ALL BEGAN
Tex finds and shelters an Indian boy and is rewarded with four magic feathers.

### 2. KIDNAPPED
Pedro and Fernando take 'Doc' Haggety hostage.

### 3. PEDRO HAS A PLAN
Pedro and Fernando plan to rid themselves of the sheriff.

### 4. PEDRO'S PARDON
Pedro decides to 'go straight' and become respectable.

### 5. SHERIFF FOR A DAY
Tex is called away and lends his magic guns to Little Jake.

### 6. INDIAN ATTACK
Pedro and Fernando try to steal Tex's magic feathers

### 7. A CLOSE SHAVE
Pedro and Fernando plot again to foil the sheriff.

### 8. DUSTY BECOMES DEPUTY
Pedro and Fernando aim to rob the bank while Tex is away.

### 9. GUN RUNNERS
Tex and Dusty go in search of villains selling guns to Indians.

### 10. TROUBLE IN YELLOW GULCH
Pedro and Fernando hold Four Feather Falls to ransom.

### 11. FRAME-UP
Tex rides off alone into the desert, unaware of a ghostly legend.

### 12. GOLD DIGGERS
Pedro and Fernando ask to spend the night in Tex's jail.

### 13. GOLD IS WHERE YOU FIND IT
Pedro and Fernando try to swindle the people of Four |Feather Falls out of their savings.

### 14. TRAPPED
Jake and his Indian friend are trapped in caves.

### 15. THE BEST LAID SCHEMES
Pedro and Fernando think they have found the solution to dealing with the sheriff.

### 16. ESCORT
Pedro and Fernando hear about the arrival of a shipment of gold in Four Feather Falls

### 17. THE TOUGHEST GUY IN THE WEST
Grandpa Twink has the chance to prove himself against real live Indians.

## 18. GHOST OF A CHANCE
Tex has to help exorcise a haunted gold mine.

## 19. GUNPLAY
Tex is challenged to a shoot-out by some cattle rustlers.

## 20. A LAWMAN RIDES ALONE
Tex goes alone to capture two wanted stage coach robbers.

## 21. JAIL BREAK
Pedro and Fernando try to claim a $500 reward.

## 22. A LITTLE BIT O' LUCK
While Tex is away, robbers raid the town bank.

## 23. LAND GRABBERS
Tex is in danger when attempts are made to force his friend to sell his land.

## 24. ONCE A LAWMAN
Tex has to find an audacious thief who has robbed the bank three times.

## 25. ELECTION DAY
Pedro tries to prevent Tex's re-election as sheriff.

## 26. GUNFIGHT ON MAIN STREET
A friend of Tex's seeks revenge on the gunmen who shot his brother.

## 27. A BAD NAME
Tex's friend, Ben, is framed for cattle rustling.

## 28. THE MA JONES STORY
Two strangers try to put Ma Jones out of business.

## 29. HORSE THIEVES
Pedro and Fernando put Tex's horse, Rocky, in danger.

## 30. BANDITS ABROAD
Pedro and Fernando try to get the $200 reward for the capture of a bandit.

### 31. A CURE FOR EVERYTHING
A medicine man poses a problem for 'Doc' Haggety.

### 32. TEETHING TROUBLES
Tex has totrick Rocky into visiting a dentist.

### 33. FIRST TRAIN THROUGH
An avalanche threatens the new railroad in Four Feather Falls.

### 34. BUFFALO ROCKY
Tex and Rocky track down a thief who's been stealing the town's mail..

### 35. SAFE AS HOUSES
Tex and the town bank manager have to reassure the townsfolk of the safety of their money.

### 36. HAPPY BIRTHDAY
The people of Four Feather Falls throw a birthday party for Tex.

### 37. FANCY SHOOTIN'
Tex has to deal with an escaped gunman when the circus comes to town.

### 38. RIDE 'EM COWBOY
Tex is challenged to ride in the rodeo for a new pair of boots.

### 39. AMBUSH
Indians steal the railroad payroll and Tex and Rocky must go into action.

**Voices**

Tex Tucker ... Nicholas Parsons
Tex Tucker (singing) ...
Michael Holliday
Rocky/Dusty/Pedro ...
Kenneth Connor
Grandpa Twink/ Fernando ...
David Graham
Ma Jones/ Little Jake ... Denise Bryer

**Principal credits**
An AP Films Production for Granada TV
39 fifteen minute episodes
Black and white
Producer: Gerry Anderson
Director: Gerry Anderson
Special effects: Reg Hill
Songs: Michael Holliday

1961

Supercar - a futuristic multi-terrain vehicle, a one-of-a-kind experimental model, used by the scientists who invented it and their test-pilot in numerous exciting adventures. From its isolated laboratory base in the middle of the Nevada desert, the technologically astounding Supercar travels the world - by land, air sea or space!

Supercar has eight rockets which can be controlled from a distance by a special remote control. On land it hovers just above the surface. When under water, it has a periscope and sonar. Its' unique 'clearvu' system allows the pilot to 'see' on a display screen in the cockpit through clouds, fog or storms.

## Characters

MIKE MERCURY - the fearless and courageous test pilot who flies Supercar
DOCTOR BEAKER and PROFESSOR POPKISS - co-inventors of Supercar, helping Mike Mercury out when they can, and inventing new accessories for the vehicle
JIMMY GIBSON - a 10 year old boy rescued by Supercar who became part of the team
MITCH - Jimmy's pet monkey
MASTERSPY - the evil villain out to steal Supercar at any opportunity
ZARIN - Masterspy's and bungling accomplice

## 1. RESCUE

Bill and Jimmy Gibson run into trouble when their plane crashes into the sea and their dinghy becomes enveloped in thick fog. Professor Popkiss, working on his new experimental craft - Supercar - refuses to allow his test pilot to go out and rescue the pair. He eventually

relents and Mike Mercury is able to use Supercar's Clear-vu to see right through the mist and is able to rescue Bill, Jimmy and his pet monkey, Mitch.

## 2. AMAZONIAN ADVENTURE

Mitch is ill and the only cure is a plant, the T'logi, which is found solely in remote parts of South America. When Mike Mercury and Dr Beaker fly off in Supercar to the Amazon, they are captured by headhunting tribesmen. Mike manages to escape and with the help of Supercar's mighty engines and some 'white magic' fireworks by Beaker, the tribesmen are convinced that he is not mortal and pay homage to him with the very precious plant they had come for.

## 3. TALISMAN OF SARGON

Masterspy, disguised as Dr Meternick, tricks Beaker into transcribing an ancient tablet which reveals the entrance to the Tomb of Sargon, wherein lies the priceless jewel, the Talisman of Sargon, which is reputed to have magic powers. Masterspy and Zarin plan to use the gem to overthrow the local ruler, Mustapha Bey. When Supercar and Mike Mercury arrive, Masterspy traps them in a tomb, and it is up to Mitch to free them and save the day.

## 4. FALSE ALARM

In a plan to steal Supercar, Masterspy and Zarin send out a phoney call for

help from some trapped mountaineers. Beaker and Mike set out to rescue them, but while camping at the foot of the mountains they are drugged and Masterspy and Zarin take off with their prize. Back at the lab, Mitch switches on the radio, alerting the team to the theft. When the villains refuse to land, Mitch is allowed to give them a rough ride using the remote control. The two sick men give up and Mike Mercury takes control again.

## 5. WHAT GOES UP

Beaker and Popkiss are helping Colonel Lewis of the USAF to test a new rocket fuel. Things go wrong when the test balloon, carrying the highly explosive fuel, goes out of control and all efforts to detonate the load fails. Mike must risk his life by firing at the balloon at very close range. After repairing a leak in the pressurised cabin of Supercar, Mike is able to explode the fuel and escape the devastating result using the mighty speed of Supercar.

## 6. KEEP IT COOL

Bill Gibson and Beaker are transporting new experimental Supercar fuel across the Nevada desert at night. Masterspy causes them to crash their truck and, after capturing them, sets out with the fuel - ignoring Beaker's warning that it will explode if its temperature rises above freezing point. Masterspy smashes their radio, so Mike cannot locate them and deliver the new batteries for the refrigeration system. However, the ultimate explosion of the fuel provides an ideal beacon for Mike.

## 7. GROUNDED

Harper and Judd steal Beaker's printed circuits for Supercar's new remote control and communication console, designed by Beaker and J. Fairleigh Prothero, of A.P. Electronics. Harper tells the team when and where he will leave the country, but when Mike sets off in Supercar, he crashes - the result of sabotage by Harper. Supercar can still travel as a car and, for the first time, Mike continues the chase by road, arriving at the airport ahead of Harper

and Judd - and retrieves the precious circuit.

## 8. JUNGLE HAZARD

Masterspy attempts to take an estate in Malaya from Miss Felicity Farnsworth for its valuable rubber. Unknown to him, she is a cousin of Beaker, and when she writes to him about the arrival of Mr Smith and Mr Zarin, the team realises she is in trouble. Mike and Beaker set

off in Supercar and are only just in time to prevent Masterspy from cutting away a flimsy rope bridge across a crocodile infested swamp and killing Miss Farnsworth. Mike is able to lift her clear by using a coil of wire.

## 9. HIGH TENSION

Another Masterspy scheme to get Supercar, this time by kidnapping Beaker. All seems lost until Mike hits upon the idea of sending Supercar to the rendezvous point on remote control. But first Mike will fly it to a spot nearby and while Masterspy is engaged, will rescue his friend. All goes according to plan, and Beaker even puts a finishing touch to the plan by telling Popkiss and Jimmy to press a taped-over button in the lab. It electrifies the hull of Supercar, giving a nasty shock!

## 10. A LITTLE ART

Beaker buys a painting, little knowing it is a visual clue to the location of an infamous forger's counterfeit plates. An attempt to find the plates by an art dealer, after he steals back the painting, fails as Beaker has sprayed a solvent on it which dissolves the top layer as he thinks there is an Old Master underneath. Meanwhile, the team accidentally discover the true meaning

of the painting and armed with photographs of the forger's paintings successfully find the plates.

## 11. ICE FALL

The team go on a trip to the mountains, but Beaker gets into trouble when he sets off to find some ice falls in an underground cavern. Mitch accidentally spoils his plans of marking his path with string. It is up to him to lead Mike in Supercar to where Beaker is trapped - encased in ice after causing an ice fall with his excited shouting at his discoveries. Mike frees the Doctor by melting the ice around him with the Supercar's engines.

## 12. ISLAND INCIDENT

The Supercar team are asked for help by the deposed but peaceful ruler of Pelota. His brother has seized power and is bringing a reign of terror to the island. Mike takes Supercar and uses the Clear-vu to survey General Humberto's headquarters, but is spotted and fired

upon. Mike and the real President next attempt to land by going underwater, and after being able to negotiate the anti-submarine nets, land onshore and expose the evil brother for what he is.

## 13. THE TRACKING OF MASTERSPY

Masterspy poses as a reporter and tricks Mike into giving him information about Supercar. He steals the plans to the machine, but not before being tricked into taking what he thinks is a new top secret project of Beaker's - really a tracking device. With the damage Masterspy has done to the amplifier apparatus of Supercar, Mike sets off after the crook and with the threat of calling in the police, persuades him and Zarin to hand back the stolen plans.

## 14. PHANTOM PIPER

The team fly over 7,000 miles to Scotland to help Miss Farnsworth solve the mystery of the Phantom Piper. They discover he is real enough by using the Clear-vu and that the piping is to disguise the noise of someone filing away an iron grille in the castle cellar. The next night they set a trap and discover the 'piper' is Harper, using a tape recorder, and his accomplice in the cellar is Judd. Further investigations reveal a fortune hidden behind the grille.

## 15. DEEP SEVEN

Supercar is to be tested underwater to see what depths it can reach. With Bill Gibson and Beaker on the shore, Mike takes the craft 400 feet down to the seabed. Suddenly, the cockpit leaks and the engines are affected. Beaker tells Mike what he must do, and soon he has restored power, only to be caught up in a mine cable. Bill Gibson dons his diving suit and goes down to try and free

Supercar before the mine explodes. The tests prove, ultimately, to be a success.

## 16. PIRATE PLUNDER

Black Morgan is a pirate, holding up ships and stealing their riches. The team set a decoy vessel to trap him and, with Mike submerged nearby, the pirate attacks the bait ship with his friends on board. The pirate warns he will fire his homing torpedoes if they try to follow, but Mike doesn't know this and attacks. A torpedo is fired, but Beaker - refusing to abandon ship - deflects it just in time. Mike attacks the pirate ship from the air and captures Morgan.

## 17. FLIGHT OF FANCY

Jimmy dreams that he and Mitch (who can talk) fly off in Supercar and rescue a princess from two scheming politicians, Hertz and Marzak. Just in time, they are able to fly off to the capital and stop the two evil men from deposing the King. As a reward, Jimmy and his pet are knighted. As this happens, Jimmy wakes up and discovers he has been dreaming, that Mitch can no longer talk and that the 'real' princess is safe and sound.

## 18. HOSTAGE

While on holiday in Ireland, Beaker is involved in a kidnapping plot staged by Judd and Harper. They kidnap an inn keeper's daughter, Eileen O'Farrell, and Beaker is forced to send for Mike Mercury and Supercar. They try to outwit the two crooks, but they themselves become the subject of a trap, and Supercar is nearly blown to pieces until saved by Popkiss and his remote control. He pilots the machine back to Ireland and manages to save Mike and Eileen from being blown up. Mitch uses a baseball bat to teach the crooks a lesson!

## 19. THE SUNKEN TEMPLE

While helping Professor Terman with his underwater excavations Mike and Beaker find a safe containing the stolen loot of a crook, Spyros, hidden beneath a huge statue on the seabed. Spyros tampers with Terman's air supply, but Mike saves him in Supercar. Terman decides to dive alone one night, but becomes trapped beneath the statue. Popkiss uses Supercar's engines to free him, while Mike and Beaker prevent Spyros from firing at the craft with his homemade torpedoes.

## 20. TRAPPED IN THE DEPTHS

An American officer and Australian scientist are trapped at the bottom of the sea in an experimental bathyscape after being attacked by a giant fish. Mike and Beaker set off to rescue them, and after being attacked themselves by the fish and using Supercar's ultrasonic gun to scare off the monster, they successfully free the two men. Mike then pilots the craft to the surface and into the air - another successful rescue!

## 21. CRASH LANDING

Supercar crashes in the jungle, with Mike, Beaker, Jimmy and Mitch aboard. Beaker makes repairs but when Popkiss, at the lab, tests the craft on remote control, the noise it creates causes a herd of elephants to stampede. An air attack forces them away from the team. Meanwhile, Mitch has disappeared and Jimmy eventually finds him with a female monkey. After much heartache, Mitch finally decides to go back with Jimmy. It isn't until they are back at the lab that they discover a stowaway - the female monkey!

## 22. THE DRAGON OF HO MENG

Forced down by a typhoon, Mike, Jimmy and Mitch come across Ho Meng and his daughter, Lotus Blossom, who look upon Supercar as a dragon. Mike takes Ho Meng for a ride which rids him of his fears. Ho Meng and Lotus Blossom are the caretakers of an ancient temple, but soon Mike, Jimmy, Mitch and the girl are imprisoned in it by Mr Fang who plans to blow it up while in

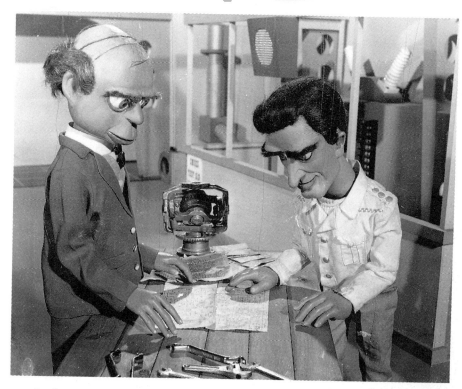

search of treasure. Mitch comes to the rescue - he finds an escape route and foils Mr Fang's plans by tampering with the explosives.

## 23. THE LOST CITY

Professor Watkins, a mad Englishman, has a plan to destroy Washington with a guided missile from his hideout beneath a lost city. Beaker and Mike are captured when they stumble across the city and Jimmy nearly ends up the same way, but Supercar's engines manage to destroy the Professor's robot. Mike and Beaker escape by imitating Watkins' voice, and it is up to Beaker to use his radio to deflect the missile back to its home base beneath the lost city in the Amazon.

## 24. MAGIC CARPET

The team fly to Central Asia with some urgent medical supplies for the dying Prince Hassan. Alif Bey wants him to die so that he can seize power, so the team are thrown into a prison tower. By using the pocket-sized remote control, they are able to fly Supercar to the Princess and she is able to give Hassan the medicine. Mitch escapes and brings back a file and the team are able to escape, leaving a puzzled guard who

keeps seeing Supercar flying, but the crew locked up.

## 25. THE WHITE LINE

Scotland Yard call in the Supercar team to help solve a series of bank and armoured car robberies. The team discover that two Chicago gangsters, Joe and Maxie Hoyle, are behind it all and soon Beaker is sent out with an armoured car as bait. Mike and Supercar are nearly captured by the Hoyles, but Mitch helps them escape and they race to help Beaker who is nearly caught in their trap of faked road lines. In their panic to escape, the Hoyles are caught in their own trap!

## 26. SUPERCAR: TAKE ONE

While Popkiss is on holiday Beaker plays with his new toy - a movie camera. His exposed film is mixed up with some film shot by spies. The team fly to New York to capture the spies, Herman Gredenski and Olma. Mike and Beaker find themselves trapped in a room filling with gas. But Beaker's bowler hat is a radio and his umbrella a drill, and Jimmy is contacted to call the police while Beaker drills out. Mitch ends the adventure by catching the agents with their own trap-door.

## 1. THE RUNAWAY TRAIN

Beaker and Popkiss are aboard a new atomic powered train, but danger is soon near as they learn that Masterspy and Zarin have sabotaged the reactor which will cause the train to crash. Mike confronts Masterspy with Supercar, but he tells him he cannot stop the train. When all seems lost, Mike is able to swoop over the express and using a new magnetic grab device, together with the Supercar's mighty engines, is able to bring the runaway train to a halt. Beaker is saved by his own invention.

## 2. PRECIOUS CARGO

Popkiss wants some wine for his cooking and his sister Heidi recommends a French wine merchant named Monsieur Laval. He is the guardian of a French girl, Zizi, who longs to escape his unkind and hard ways. She dreams of Jimmy and Supercar. Laval sends a crate of wine ordered by Popkiss. But the crate contains more than wine when it arrives at Black Rock - Zizi has stowed away. They can't send her back, so Aunt Heidi agrees to look after her.

## 3. OPERATION SUPERSTORK

Mitch unties the guide ropes to a new balloon, which Beaker has built, sending Mike, Jimmy and Beaker into danger. In a terrible storm, Mike bails out with the only parachute and returns to rescue them by hooking Supercar's aerial over the limp balloon, just as the last of the air runs out. So despite Mitch's mischief, Mike and Supercar are once again able to come to the rescue and save the day.

## 4. HI-JACK

Masterspy and Zarin plan to hi-jack an airliner piloted by Bill Gibson and with Beaker and Jimmy aboard. Bill is forced at gunpoint to head for the islands of Bantonga, where the aircraft will be handed over to President Gourmet, who is in the employ of Masterspy. Beaker and Jimmy are able to radio Mike back at base and tell of their plight with the words, "Hi-jack!" Mike takes off in Supercar and buzzes the President's plane en route to meet Bill Gibson's aircraft forcing him to call off the attack.

## 5. CALLING CHARLIE QUEEN

Mike and Beaker answer a distress call from an amateur radio 'ham'. The caller is Karloff, who plans to take over America by miniaturising its citizens. Mike and Beaker are both miniaturised and only just manage, with the help of the Professor's miniature assistant, to make up an antidote to restore them to full size. The same fate is suffered by Popkiss and Jimmy, who have come to find their friend. Karloff is finally given a taste of his own medicine!

## 6. SPACE FOR MITCH

Mitch lands himself in trouble again with his tricks; this time he sets off a rocket which the team have been working on. Off he goes - into orbit! His air is running out, so Mike takes off in Supercar to rescue him. He uses the retro rockets to slow the capsule down and force it back into the atmosphere. Mitch, somewhat bewildered, goes falling towards the Earth, but the capsule's parachutes open and it lands safely in the sea. Mike then lifts it home and Mitch is safe.

## 7. THE SKY'S THE LIMIT

Masterspy and Zarin want Supercar; they try to buy it using phoney money. When this fails they enlist the help of two thugs, Jazz and Bud, to steal the craft. Meanwhile, Beaker discovers he has invented a paint which makes things invisible. Masterspy attacks the Nevada Desert base and, following a gun battle, is allowed to enter the launch bay. He finds nothing; Supercar _is_ there but Beaker has covered it with his paint, making it completely invisible.

## 8. 70 - B - LO

Popkiss needs a blood transfusion, but he has a rare blood group and the nearest compatible donor, Professor Karsinsky, is trapped by bad weather in the Arctic. Mike takes off in Supercar

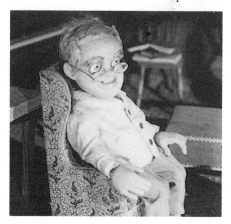

with Dr Maslin, but when they arrive they are threatened by Jason, the Professor's assistant. The two men have discovered uranium and Jason wants to sell the news to the highest bidder. Beaker, at the base, uses the remote control to stop Jason using Supercar for his escape.

## 9. ATOMIC WITCH HUNT

Atomic bombs have been planted all over the United States. The Supercar team set out to discover who is behind the plot and find submarines which disappear into a cave off the Gulf Coast. Beaker, Mitch and Mike are captured by the gang, and so too is Jimmy - by the local sheriff, the leader of the gang. Mitch saves the day when he is able to stop the sheriff and his men in their evil scheme.

## 10. JAIL BREAK

Red James plans to free his friend Joe Anna from prison by using a helicopter. The head of the helicopter company, Sam Weston, is forced to fly the 'chopper' and Anna is freed. James spots the Black Rock base of Supercar and forces Mike at gunpoint to pilot them in Supercar to New Mexico. Beaker's new ejector seat in Supercar lets Mike escape and the craft is landed by remote control. A gun battle follows, but the crooks are eventually overpowered.

## 11. THE DAY TIME STOOD STILL

Mike dreams of his birthday party, with all his friends - Beaker, Popkiss, Jimmy, Mitch, Zizi and Aunt Heidi. Suddenly, all his friends stop, as if time itself is frozen. A stranger in long, flowing robes appears. He is from another planet and is there to present Mike with an award for his promotion of peace and goodwill. He gives Mike a sash and magic belt which allows him to fly up and out of the workshop roof and into the sky. Suddenly, he plummets back to

Earth and wakes up! It has all been a dream and the team are there for his party.

## 12. TRANSATLANTIC CABLE

Masterspy is tapping a transatlantic cable from an old wreck on the seabed. The Supercar team find the wreck but don't believe Jimmy when he says he saw a light coming from it. They later change their minds and Mike uses a new Supercar device, a large twist drill, to plunge a hole in the wreck and force out Masterspy's frogmen.

## 13. KING KOOL

When Dr. Beaker pays a visit to Batesville, Mitch is tricked by King Kool, a famous TV gorilla and jazz drummer, and finds himself locked up in his cage. King Kool travels back to the laboratory, hiding as Mitch did, and the team can only think that Mitch has somehow turned into a giant. Bud Haberger, TV show host, thinks King Kool has shrunk when he sees Mitch in the cage. The error is soon realised and Mike flies the gorilla back, but only

after Bud promises not to lock up King Kool in his cage again.

### Voices
Mike Mercury...Graydon Gould
Doctor Beaker...David Graham
Mitch the Monkey...David Graham
Professor Popkiss...George Murcell
Masterspy...George Murcell
Zarin...David Graham
Jimmy Gibson...Sylvia Anderson
Other female voices...Sylvia Anderson

### Principal Credits
39 thirty minute episodes
Black and white
An AP Films Production for ITC
World-Wide Distribution
Scripts : Reg Hill, Gerry & Sylvia Anderson, Hugh and Martin Woodhouse
Music Composer and Director : Barry Gray
Director of Photography : John Read
Special Effects : Derek Meddings
Puppeteers : Christine Glanville, Mary Turner and others

1962

In the year 2067, the fantastic spaceship Fireball XL5 is just one of the World Space Patrol's roving vehicles and its crew is responsible for Sector 25 of space. As they patrol the galaxy, encountering many alien races, and occasionally extra-terrestrial or human villains, such as the Green Men, the Subterrains and Mr and Mrs Space Spy, Steve Zodiac and his team use the many capabilities of their craft to aid them in preserving peace, before returning home to Space City.

## Characters

COLONEL STEVE ZODIAC - the dynamic pilot of Fireball XL5

PROFESSOR MATTHEW "MATT" MATIC - XL5's bespectacled navigator and scientific officer

VENUS - the crew's medical expert and Steve's romantic interest

ZOONIE - Venus's pet, a 'Lazoon'

ROBERT THE ROBOT - Steve's faithful co-pilot , a transparent robot

COMMANDER ZERO - along with his assistant Lieutenant Ninety he supervises Space City (XL5's base), and all Fireball missions

## 1. PLANET 46

*Script by Sylvia Anderson*
*Directed by Gerry Anderson*

A planetomic missile, capable of destroying the world, has been fired from Planet 46. The crew of Fireball XL5, on their way home, destroy the missile and head for Planet 46, where Steve Zodiac and Venus are captured by the Green Men - the Subterrains, who seek to destroy Earth. With Venus hostage, they launch another missile, but Steve manages to escape and takes the leader of the Subterrains with him. He is able to rescue Venus and destroy the missile before it reaches Earth.

## 2. HYPNOTIC SPHERE

*Script by Alan Fennell*
*Directed by Alan Pattillo*

Several space tankers have been put out of action, their pilots in a hypnotic trance. The crew of Fireball XL5 escort another tanker, and themselves become victims of an hypnotic light and voice. Robert the Robot is immune and takes control of the spacecraft. The crew again fly the same route, this time blocking out the light, and discover that the menace is coming from a huge brain cell, like an octopus. It needs heat to live and Steve manages to overcome the

hypnotic power and destroy its heating plant.

## 3. PLANET OF PLATONIA

*Script by Alan Fennell*
*Directed by David Ellicott*

Steve and Venus, together with Robert the Robot, land in Fireball Junior on the Platinum Planet, to take the King up to the orbiting Fireball XL5 and on to Earth for trade talks. Volvo, aide to the King, wishes to go to war with Earth and plants a bomb inside Robert. He refuses to reveal to Steve where the bomb is, so Steve takes him along on the journey back to Earth. Volvo is forced to reveal where he planted the bomb and Steve is able to remove it and eject it into space.

## 4. SPACE MAGNET

*Script by Anthony Marriott*
*Directed by Bill Harris*

Fireball XL5 is sent to investigate the disappearance of Fireball XL7. The Moon is pulled out of orbit and XL5 is taken with it to Planet Magneton which has the most powerful gravitational pull in the Universe. They discover a huge power house, being fed by a giant electro-magnet on a crane - with pieces of Fireball XL7. The invisible people of

the planet, the Solars, plan to pull the Moon into their orbit and bring light into their dark world. Steve overcomes them with his ray gun, reverses the power and sends the Moon back into its Earth orbit.

## 5. THE DOOMED PLANET

*Script by Alan Fennell*
*Directed by Alan Pattillo*

A flying saucer leads the crew of XL5 to Membrono, a planet doomed to be destroyed by another planet which has come out of its orbit. An old man sent the saucer to lure Steve Zodiac to Membrono where, through Robert, he asks him to use Fireball's powerful missiles to destroy the drifting planet before it destroys Membrono and in turn his own world, which is governed by it. Hearing this, Steve is able to help the old man and save his peaceful world.

## 6. PLANT MAN FROM SPACE

*Script by Anthony Marriott*
*Directed by John Kelly*

A missile from space lands at Space City, but doesn't explode, but instead a strange, quick-growing plant covers the place. Hormone from the planet Hedera will destroy it, but when the crew of XL5, along with Dr Rootes, who has just arrived after experimenting with plants in space, land on the planet they are met by a 'plant man' - the creation of Rootes, who has become obsessed with plant life. Robert the Robot must come to the rescue.

## 7. THE SUN TEMPLE

*Script by Anthony Marriott*
*Directed by John Kelly*

Sun worshippers, the Rejuscans, fear that missiles from Space City, being used to destroy dangerous meteorites will anger their god. They destroy the launch site at Space City and when the crew of Fireball XL5 land on their planet in Fireball Junior to investigate, they capture Venus and attempt to kill her by strapping her to the altar in their sun temple, in the path of the sun's rays. Steve Zodiac and Zoonie are just in time to rescue her.

## 8. SPACE IMMIGRANTS

*Script by Anthony Marriott*
*Directed by Alan Pattillo*

Venus and Jock, the Space City Engineer, are taking a team to New Earth, aboard the Mayflower III, where they hope to set up equipment to make the planet suitable for human life. The tiny and evil inhabitants of the planet, the Lillispations, plan to prevent this and are able to trick Venus by imitating the voice of Steve Zodiac. They make Robert destroy the ship's oxygen pills - needed to save Jock's life, but Steve becomes suspicious and goes in XL5 to the planet. Zoonie soon has them captured and Steve is able to save Venus and other patrol members.

## 9. SPACE MONSTER

*Script by Gerry and Sylvia Anderson*
*Directed by John Kelly*

Fireball XL2 has disappeared and the crew of XL5 are sent to find it. They receive a distress call from the planet Monotane, where Steve and Venus, landing in Fireball Junior, find the wreckage of XL2. A storm forces them into a cave where they find the crew of the destroyed ship, who tell them a

monster caused the crash and is now outside the cave. Professor Matic lands in Fireball XL5 and is also forced into the cave. Steve tries to escape but it is up to Zoonie to save the day by imitating the sound of the monster.

## 10. FLYING ZODIAC

*Script by Anthony Marriott*
*Directed by Bill Harris*

A circus visits Space City and the special guests are Madame Mivea and Cosmo the Clown - really Mr and Mrs Space Spy in disguise. They plan to use the circus to allow the Nomadians to take over Earth to provide a home for them. Steve Zodiac's trapeze wires are tampered with and, when they snap, Jock just manages to save him by shooting out of a cannon and grabbing his dangling ankles! The Nomadian leader captures Lieutenant Ninety, but just when things seem lost, one of Professor Matic's experiments explodes and Venus wakes up. It was all a dream!

## 11. XL5 TO H2O

*Script by Alan Fennell*
*Directed by John Kelly*

Fireball XL5 is sent to help the two survivors of a planet who are being attacked by a fish man, armed with a poisonous smoke gun. The crew arrive to find the glass city of the planet destroyed, and no sign of the survivors. The fish man attacks, but is driven off. They find the survivors in an underground shelter, but the creature attacks again. Steve and Venus are just able to drag the survivors away from the poisonous fumes of the smoke gun and Steve then uses his stun gun to overcome the beast.

## 12. A SPY IN SPACE

*Script by Alan Fennell*
*Directed by Alan Pattillo*

Fireball XL5 is asked to take over the patrol duty of XL9, which has been attacked and damaged. The crew make their way to the nearest space station to refuel, but find it empty. Mr and Mrs Space Spy have taken over the station and plan to use Venus as a hostage to steal XL5. Their ship, the S.S. Thor, was responsible for the attack on XL9. All seems lost until a rocket is placed in the sole of Mr Space Spy's magnetic

boots, sending him into orbit. Mrs Space Spy takes the S.S. Thor to rescue him.

## 13. SPACE PIRATES

*Script by Anthony Marriott*
*Directed by Bill Harris*

Space Pirates, based on the planet Aridan, are holding up freighters from nearby planet Minera. Steve Zodiac plans to take a spacecraft and trick the pirates into thinking it's another helpless freighter. The pirates overhear this and manage to knock Steve out. Robert is sent back to Space City as proof that they are holding Steve as hostage. Professor Matic and Venus deliver fresh water supplies to the pirates, but they are drugged. Steve is released - but it was all just a bedtime story told to Jonathan Zero!

## 14. CONVICT IN SPACE

*Script by Alan Fennell*
*Directed by Bill Harris*

Grothan Deblis, the spy, steals some top secret plans, but is captured by the crew of XL5 and sentenced to twenty years imprisonment on the prison planet

Deblis takes them to the volcanic planet Voldanda where he has hidden the plans. He double-crosses Mr and Mrs Spy and Steve is able to rescue Professor Matic and recapture Deblis.

## 15. SPACE PEN

*Script by Dennis Spooner*
*Directed by John Kelly*

Two crooks manage to steal isotopes from Space City. The crew of XL5 go after them to the Planet Conva, but find trouble there. Steve tricks the crooks into thinking that he and his crew are also villains and have stolen XL5. But the leaders of the gang are Mr and Mrs Space Spy, who recognize the crew of XL5 and order their death in a water chamber. The controller of the planet, General Shan, is able to rescue the crew and capture Mr and Mrs Space Spy.

## 16. THE LAST OF THE ZANADUS

*Script by Anthony Marriott*
*Directed by Alan Pattillo*

Kudos, the last inhabitant of the planet Zanadu, is determined to kill all Lazoons. He uses Major Jim Ireland, an

crew of XL5, along with Ireland, go to the planet, stun Kudos and give the antidote to Zoonie. Kudos' spell of eternal life is broken and he becomes an old man.

## 17. THE WINGS OF DANGER

*Script by Alan Fennell*
*Directed by David Ellicott*

Subterrains One and Two plan to use a robot bird , fitted with deadly radium capsules, to kill Steve Zodiac in revenge for the capture of their leader. They send out radio signals from Planet 46, which the crew of XL5 check out. Steve becomes ill and Venus finds a tiny capsule of radium in him. The robot bird tries again to kill him, but Steve is able to use a stun gun to damage it. A high-pitched noise is heard - the same as the one that came from Planet 46. Steve threatens to use the bird on the Subterrains, but they agree to remain peaceful.

## 18. THE TRIADS

*Script by Alan Fennell*
*Directed by Alan Pattillo*

Nuclear explosions are coming from the planet Triad and Fireball XL5 is sent to investigate. They crash land in Fireball Junior and find that they have run out of fuel. They find themselves in a giant jungle and are forced into the trees by a giant tiger. They are rescued by two giants, Graff and Snaff, who tell them that their experimental rocket fuel keeps exploding, causing the nuclear explosions. Their fuel is the problem and the XL5 team are able to alter it and use it to refuel Fireball Junior.

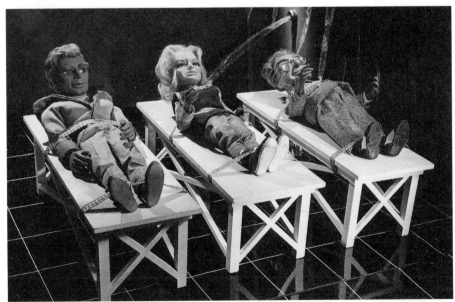

Conva. Mr and Mrs Space Spy trick Steve Zodiac and capture Professor Matic to force Steve to hand over Deblis, whom they plan to trick into revealing the whereabouts of the plans.

explorer, to give Zoonie the deadly milomytosis virus. Steve realizes that Ireland must be responsible and forces him to reveal the antidote - water from the Fountain of Life on Zanadu. The

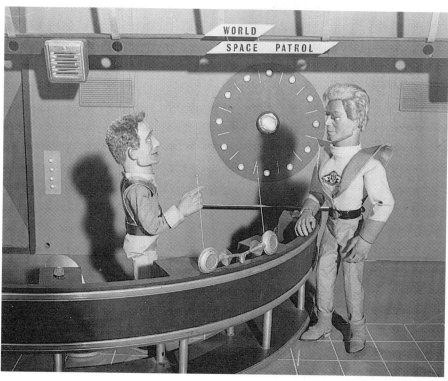

## 19. SABOTAGE
*Script by Anthony Marriott*
*Directed by John Kelly*

A bomb planted aboard Fireball XL5 sends the spaceship out of control. Ultra Arcon and Arcon Commander, from the planet Electron, move in with the Gamma Spaceship and use their gamma ray to transport the crew of XL5 to their craft and then to their planet. Steve finds a pair of Arcon glasses which protect the wearer from gamma rays. They escape, stealing the Gamma Spaceship. Steve is forced to use the gamma ray on Commander Zero who is about to attack their stolen spaceship.

## 20. PRISONER ON THE LOST PLANET
*Script by Anthony Marriott*
*Directed by Bill Harris*

The crew of XL5 land on a misty planet in response to a distress call. Steve Zodiac, on his jetmobile, finds a beautiful woman Aphros, who tells him she has been exiled to the planet and wants to go to Earth. When Steve tells her this isn't possible, she drugs him and threatens to activate the volcano that is nearby. Professor Matic fires an interceptor at the cave where Steve is

held prisoner, thus enabling him to escape and take Aphros prisoner. Holding her in the Space jail, they return home.

## 21. FLIGHT TO DANGER
*Script by Alan Fennell*
*Directed by David Ellicott*

Lieutenant Ninety is trying to win his astronaut wings and his final test is a solo orbit of the Moon, but something goes wrong and his capsule explodes. He ejects just in time, but the crew of

XL5 can't find him. Just as they are about to return to Earth, Professor Matic picks him up on his Spacemascope and Steve is able to rescue him. In the sick bay of XL5 he is presented with his wings by Commander Zero.

## 22. SPACE VACATION
*Script by Dennis Spooner*
*Directed Alan Pattillo*

Steve Zodiac, Venus and Matic arrive on the beautiful planet Olympus for a holiday. At a birthday party given by Jankel, chief of Olympus, for his son Ergon, his enemy Kanerick - ruler of the dark planet Kemble - poisons the boy and takes Venus hostage back to Kemble. Venus is the only one who can save Ergon, and Jankel forces Steve to rescue her by holding Matic hostage. This he does, but they are only just able to battle through a violent storm to get back to Olympus to administer the antidote.

## 23. MYSTERY OF THE TA2
*Script by Dennis Spooner*
*Directed by John Kelly*

The crew of Fireball XL5 discover the

wreckage of TA2, a spaceship which disappeared fifty years before. A map found in the wreckage reveals that the pilot, Colonel Denton, intended to go to the planet Arctan after ejecting. On the planet the crew are captured by two ice men and put on trial for trying to steal their king - Denton! He orders their release and, when Steve Zodiac offers to take him back to Earth, he does not accept.

## 24. ROBERT TO THE RESCUE
*Script by Dennis Spooner*
*Directed by Bill Harris*

The XL5 crew are sent to investigate a new planet which suddenly appears and then disappears. Fireball XL5 is pulled across the planet, and when the crew are able to leave the ship, they find that everything around them is in total darkness. A glass door in the blackness reveals a corridor, which leads to a room. Suddenly, two dome-heads, Magar and Proton, appear and tell the crew that they cannot be allowed to leave their planet and that their Earth memories will be erased. Robert is put on a conveyor belt leading to a furnace, but is able to escape and rescue the crew.

## 25. THE FORBIDDEN PLANET

*Script by Anthony Marriott*
*Directed by David Ellicott*

An ultrascope, which can look into deep space, picks up the planet Nutopia which is said to be the perfect planet. Two Nutopians use their travel transmitter to capture Professor Matic and his assistant Dr Stamp, and then Steve and Venus. On Nutopia the two aliens, Privator and Perfectos, both want to keep Venus as their eternal companion. A duel follows which leads to them both being rendered helpless, which enables Steve and his friends to return to the Space Observatory.

## 26. THE GRANATOID TANKS

*Script by Alan Fennell*
*Directed by Alan Pattillo*

Dr Baker and Dr Simpson have just finished their experiments on the glass-surfaced Planet 73. Suddenly, they discover that six Granatoid tanks - hostile robots - are coming towards the base and they send a message for help to Space City. Aboard Fireball XL5 the crew discover that Ma Doughty, owner of the Space City Music Shop, has stowed away. They reach Planet 73 and when Ma Doughty appears, the tanks retreat. She is wearing pearls made from the rare mineral plyton, the only thing the Granatoid tanks fear!

## 27. DANGEROUS CARGO

*Script by Dennis Spooner*
*Directed by John Kelly*

After surveying the derelict planet Pharos, the crew of XL5 return to Space City to be told to take some Vesivium Nine, the greatest explosive in the Universe, back to the planet and destroy it. When Steve and Professor Matic set the explosive in one of the many mines on the planet, they discover that the entrance has been blocked by the Subterrains. Robert the Robot is unable to clear the entrance, so Steve uses one of the capsules of his ray gun to clear their path. The crew are just able to leave the planet before it explodes.

## 28. 1875

*Script by Anthony Marriott*
*Directed by Bill Harris*

Steve, Venus and Commander Zero enter Professor Matic's latest invention a time machine. Suddenly, the door closes - Zoonie is playing with the controls! They find themselves back in time, in a western town. Steve becomes a Sheriff and Venus a woman bandit named Frenchie Lil, with Commander Zero as her accomplice. When Venus and Zero rob a bank, Venus is knocked unconscious. Professor Matic manages to bring Steve and Zero back, but not Venus. He increases power and just before the time machine explodes, Venus returns.

## 29. THE ROBOT FREIGHTER MYSTERY

*Script by Alan Fennell*
*Directed by David Ellicott*

Someone is sabotaging robot freighters and Commander Zero and Steve Zodiac suspect the Briggs Brothers of the Space Salvage Company. Steve discovers that Jock's new assistant, Edmundo, is planting bombs in a freighter and duly handcuffs him there. He then forces the Briggs Brothers to the freighter and handcuffs them as well. He tells them that a bomb has been put in the ship and will go off if they don't confess. With only thirteen seconds left Edmundo confesses. But the 'bomb' isn't a bomb at all - just a music box!

## 30. DRAMA AT SPACE CITY

*Script by Anthony Marriott*
*Directed by Alan Pattillo*

While Steve and Venus are on holiday, Jonathan Zero is looking after Zoonie. When, with Zoonie, he goes into the main control cabin of Fireball XL5 one

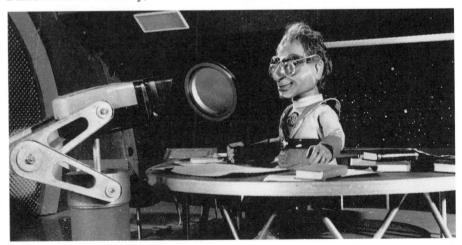

night, Zoonie gives the order, 'Full power'. Robert obeys and launches the spacecraft. This starts an alert and Commander Zero, with Lieutenant Ninety, take off after XL5 in Fireball XL1. They find it in space, on fire, and when they get aboard discover Jonathan and Zoonie unconscious. Zoonie has, however, put the fire out with a ray extinguisher.

## 31. WHISTLE FOR DANGER

*Script by Dennis Spooner*
*Directed by John Kelly*

The crew of XL5 are sent to the planet Floran to explode an Ellvium bomb in the atmosphere to kill Planitoid Three, a plant disease, so that plant life can be restored. When the bomb is exploded, two Florans manage to drug the crew and imprison them in a tower. When they try to use a tall plant as an escape route, the Florans realize that they have come to help and are able to save the crew from what is actually a man-eating plant!

## 32. FASTER THAN LIGHT

*Script by Dennis Spooner*
*Directed by Bill Harris*

When the stabilisers of XL5 break down, supplies to Space Station Nine are in jeopardy. The spacecraft travels faster than light, through the light barrier, and the crew find themselves in a sea of air and are able to repair XL5 without the use of oxygen pills. Zoonie is suddenly grabbed by a giant bird, but Steve is able to kill it with his ray gun. When they go back through the light barrier, Venus is unconscious. Rescue ships from Space City escort XL5 back to base where Venus recovers.

## 33. THE DAY THE EARTH FROZE

*Script by Alan Fennell*
*Directed by David Ellicott*

A note in the hand of an unconscious Patrol crewman leads Fireball XL5 to the ice planet Zavia. At Space City snow falls and soon everything is frozen solid. On Zavia, two icemen, Cardre and Rader, capture the crew and tell them that they plan to deflect the sun's rays using a giant reflector, thereby destroying Earth! Steve is able to use a belt buckle to chip a staircase into the wall of their ice jail, and they escape in Fireball Junior. They use a missile to destroy the giant reflector and thus save Earth.

## 34. INVASION EARTH

*Script by Dennis Spooner*
*Directed by Alan Pattillo*

Two Fireball patrol ships, sent to investigate a strange cloud in space, explode. Black spaceships emerge from the cloud and land at Space City where two aliens order Commander Zero to tell the crew of XL5 to land, although Steve is suspicious. The aliens prepare to destroy XL5 as it arrives, but suddenly they fall to the floor. Venus explains that they have the space disease Rystamesia, so Commander Zero doesn't seem quite so brave.

## 35. THE GHOSTS OF SPACE

*Script by Alan Fennell*
*Directed by John Kelly*

James Frazer, an Earth geologist, discovers electronic rock on the planet Electron. He demands that Steve Zodiac takes it back to Earth, but he refuses. Strange things happen as objects float around, but the crew of XL5 cannot discover why. When they try to leave the planet, Frazer attacks with the electronic rock, which explodes on impact. Just when it seems Steve will be hit, Frazer begins to float. Two small Groverians appear and explain that they frightened away the Electrons as they feared they would stop them taking away the electric rock. Steve gets them to apologise to the Electrons and Frazer is taken back to Earth.

## 36. TRIAL BY ROBOT

*Script by Alan Fennell*
*Directed by Bill Harris*

Robots have vanished from several planets. The only clue seems to be that Professor Himber, the greatest robot scientist in the Universe, gave a lecture when the robots were taken. After Himber has left Space City, Robert takes off in Fireball XL1. They follow him to Planet 82, where they are captured and tried by Himber for damaging an inhabitant of Robotvia. Their robot jurors find them guilty. Professor Matic is able to retune Robert and the Prosecutor Robot and after a battle with the robots, take Himber back to Earth.

### 37. THE DAY IN THE LIFE OF A SPACE GENERAL

*Script by Alan Fennell*
*Directed by David Ellicott*

Lieutenant Ninety becomes General Ninety, but things don't go very well for him. Steve Zodiac takes Jock to planet Olympus for a holiday and once there Jock is knocked out and Steve falls into a quagmire. General Ninety orders all patrol ships to intercept an invasion fleet in Sector 23 but it turns out to be a meteorite. Steve, saved by Jock, is told to land XL5 on Landing Pad 1, along with Freighter A14, but a tanker is taking off from it at the same time and XL5 crashes into Space City. Other ships explode in flames and Space City burns. Lieutenant Ninety wakes up and discovers the whole thing was only a horrible nightmare!

### 38. SPACE CITY SPECIAL

*Script by Dennis Spooner*
*Directed by Alan Pattillo*

Venus is returning to Space City aboard one of the new supersonic airliners with

General Rossiter. Major Todd, the pilot, has been brainwashed by the Subterrains and tries to crash the plane. Steve and Professor Matic in Fireball Junior manage to talk Venus down, and she is able to land the airliner safely. Back at Space City, Steve is given his award as Astronaut of the Year and Venus and the Professor are given special awards for their bravery.

### 39. THE FIRE FIGHTERS

*Script by Alan Fennell*
*Directed by John Kelly*

Balls of fire are falling all over Earth from a gas cloud in space. The crew of Fireball XL5 plan to enclose it in a giant satellite and, by injecting oxygen into it, let it burn out. With time running out, the crew successfully manage to enclose the cloud, but when they try to release the oxygen, nothing happens. If the container enters the atmosphere, Earth will become a giant fireball. Steve, using his thruster pack, is just able to release the oxygen from outside the container and get away before it explodes, leaving space clear again!

### Voices

Steve Zodiac...Paul Maxwell
Professor Matic...David Graham
Lieutenant Ninety...David Graham
Zoonie...David Graham
Venus...Sylvia Anderson
Robert the Robot...Gerry Anderson
Commander Zero...John Bluthal

### Principal Credits

39 thirty minute episodes
Black and white
An AP Films Production in association with ATV for ITC World-Wide Distribution
Producer : Gerry Anderson
Script Supervision : Gerry and Sylvia Anderson
Director of photography: John Read
Art director : Bob Bell
Special effects: Derek Meddings
Music composer, arranger and conductor : Barry Gray

1964 STINGRAY

In the year 2065, the World Aquanaut Security Patrol (W.A.S.P), operating from its base Marineville, is an organisation vital to World Security. Captained by Troy Tempest, who is responsible to Commander Sam Shore, the super-submarine Stingray patrols the seas for W.A.S.P. The vast undersea world is also in Stingray's domain - and there can be found various Aquaphibians, Terror Fish and the evil Titan!

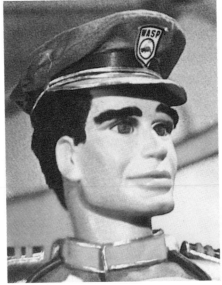

## Characters

CAPTAIN TROY TEMPEST - the heroic leader and Stingray's captain
COMMANDER SAM SHORE - the physically disabled head of WASP
PHONES - the scientific genius who accompanies Troy in Stingray
MARINA - a mute undersea girl rescued from Titan's enslavement
ATLANTA - Commander Shore's beautiful daughter
TITAN - the evil undersea lord who is the Stingray crew's fiercest enemy
AGENT X 2 ZERO - a master of disguise who is Titan's spy on land

## 1. STINGRAY

*Script by Gerry and Sylvia Anderson*
*Directed by Alan Pattillo*

Troy encounters Titan and his underwater race for the first time while investigating submarine explosions. Troy and Phones are captured by Titan and sentenced to death, but Titan's slave girl Marina helps them to escape, and herself joins WASP.

## 2. HYPNOTIC SPHERE

*Script by Alan Fennell*
*Directed by David Elliott*

When Troy takes Marina home to Pacifica, she returns with a flower for Atlanta. But X20 has made the flower poisonous, and Atlanta collapses. Troy proves Marina is innocent of the flower's deadliness, and Atlanta recovers.

## 3. SEA OF OIL

*Script by Dennis Spooner*
*Directed by John Kelly*

A race of underwater people capture Atlanta and attempt to sabotage Stingray, believing that Troy is trying to destroy their city. But Atlanta discovers the people are peace-loving, and when re-united with the Stingray crew, all misunderstandings are resolved.

## 4. HOSTAGES OF THE DEEP

*Script by Alan Fennell*
*Directed by Desmond Saunders*

A former WASP member and Marina are captured by an evil underwater inhabitant. Marina is threatened by an evil-looking swordfish, but Troy and Phones, who have been following, rescue the captives.

## 5. TREASURE DOWN BELOW

*Script by Dennis Spooner*
*Directed by Alan Pattillo*

On one of Phone's treasure hunts, Troy, Marina and Phones are captured. But Troy manages to escape, and then returns to end the careers of the underwater kidnappers and save his friends from torture.

## 6. THE BIG GUN

*Script by Alan Fennell*
*Directed by David Elliott*

Troy and Phones discover the underwater city responsible for destroying three Pacific islands. When the two surface men temporarily lose consciousness because of water pressure, Marina is forced to fire the missile that destroys the underwater city.

### 7. THE GOLDEN SEA

*Script by Dennis Spooner*
*Directed by John Kelly*

Titan attempts to destroy Stingray and a gold-mining bathyscape, using a giant electric swordfish. But Troy turns the tables on Titan by attaching the device to Titan's own craft and leaving him to his fate.

### 8. THE GHOST SHIP

*Script by Alan Fennell*
*Directed by Desmond Saunders*

An underwater creature called Idotee traps Commander Shore and Phones aboard an ancient galleon. Troy is forced to join them, but he disables Idotee by releasing laughing gas from his air cylinders.

### 9. COUNT DOWN

*Script by Dennis Spooner*
*Directed by Alan Pattillo*

X20 takes Marina prisoner by posing as a speech teacher for her, then leaves her with a bomb to destroy Marineville. But Troy discovers the plan and thwarts it with only seconds to spare.

### 10. GHOST OF THE SEA

*Script by Alan Fennell*
*Directed by David Elliott*

An oil rig has been destroyed at a place where Commander Shore once received his crippling injury and was saved by a mysterious stranger. He returns to the scene with Troy, and recognises his rescuer as the saboteur. When Troy saves the man's life, he promises to do no more damage.

### 11. EMERGENCY MARINEVILLE

*Script by Alan Fennell*
*Directed by John Kelly*

Troy, Phones and Marina are captured by enemies intent on destroying Marineville. By replacing deadly explosives with a message in the missile aimed at Marineville, Troy brings rescue and defeat of the enemy.

### 12. SUBTERRANEAN SEA

*Script by Alan Fennell*
*Directed by Desmond Saunders*

After a cancelled vacation, Troy and his crew investigate the Subterrain. But low oxygen supplies force them to hurriedly find a new shaft to the surface, where they discover a tropical island perfect for a new holiday.

### 13. THE LOCH NESS MONSTER

*Script by  Dennis Spooner*
*Directed by  Alan Pattillo*

In Loch Ness, Troy and his crew are attacked by a ferocious monster.  They destroy it in self-defence, only to discover it is a fake, a mechanism rigged up by locals to attract tourists.

### 14. THE INVADERS

*Script by  Dennis Spooner*
*Directed by  David Elliott*

An underwater race traps Troy, Phones and Marina.  Without the three knowing, a thought-reading machine tells their captors Marineville's secrets, and they are then released.  But Troy is

suspicious, and only after the Control Room is over-run by underwater men, is he able to save Marineville.

### 15. SECRET OF THE GIANT OYSTER

*Script by  Alan Fennell*
*Directed by  John Kelly*

Marina is worried by a legend of bad luck when Troy learns of an enormous pearl within a giant oyster.  Danger is averted for Stingray and its crew by the thousands of satellite oysters which also protect the giant pearl.

### 16. RAPTURE OF THE DEEP

*Script by  Alan Fennell*
*Directed by  Desmond Saunders*

Troy is living in a wonderful palace in a jewel forest.  But when the palace is attacked and he has no weapons with which to fight back.....  Troy wakes up.  It was all a dream.

### 17. STAND BY FOR ACTION

*Script by  Dennis Spooner*
*Directed by  Alan Pattillo*

Surface Agent X20 makes several attempts on Troy's life while disguised

as a producer filming WASP at work.  And when X20 turns a mock battle into a real one, Troy is needed to save all involved..... including his movie star double.

### 18. THE DISAPPEARING SHIPS

*Script by  Alan Fennell*
*Directed by  David Elliott*

Three sunken ships are to be blown up by remote control.  But when Troy discovers a sea-bed Nomad tribe living in one of the ships, he warns them, and just before the ship explodes, they escape.

## 19. MAN FROM THE NAVY

*Script by Alan Fennell*
*Directed by John Kelly*

Two Aquaphibians take over a Naval
Captain's craft while it is engaged in
mock conflict with Stingray. They fire
real missiles instead of dummies at
Stingray, then escape. Though Stingray
is unharmed, Commander Shore
believes the Naval Captain responsible
for attacking Stingray, until Troy is able
to confirm the Captain's story of
Aquaphibian saboteurs.

## 20. MARINEVILLE TRAITOR

*Script by Alan Fennell*
*Directed by Desmond Saunders*

Troy believes that Commander Shore is
a spy and jails him. But Shore has
planned this, and when the real spy
reveals himself, he is caught and the
Commander released.

## 21. TOM THUMB TEMPEST

*Script by Alan Fennell*
*Directed by Alan Pattillo*

While Troy is impatiently waiting to go
on a mission, he dozes off and dreams
that Stingray and its crew are shrunk to
miniature size and menaced by Titan.
When all seems lost, Troy reverts to
normal size - he has awoken.

## 22. PINK ICE

*Script by Alan Fennell*
*Directed David Elliott*

When the oceans of the world begin to
freeze over with pink ice, Troy is sent to
investigate. After the Stingray crew risk
death when their craft becomes trapped
in the ice, Troy locates the craft
responsible and bombards it with
missiles, ending the global threat.

## 23. THE MASTER PLAN

*Script by Alan Fennell*
*Directed by John Kelly*

An Aquaphibian poisons Troy by
shooting a cloud of purple liquid at him.

In exchange for the antidote, Marina
gives herself up to Titan. After an
instant recovery for Troy, he and Phones
must battle it out in Titanica to
free her.

## 24. STAR OF THE EAST

*Script by Alan Fennell*
*Directed by Desmond Saunders*

While in Marineville seeking WASP
membership, El Hudat, leader of an
Eastern country, is deposed, and is thus
ineligible. When he returns home, he
kidnaps Marina, but she is saved by
Troy. After regaining power, El Hudat
returns to Marineville. Commander
Shore duly enrolls him and, is able
under WASP law, to jail him.

## 25. AN ECHO OF DANGER

*Script by  Dennis Spooner*
*Directed by  Alan Pattillo*

Posing as a psychiatrist, X20 convinces Phones that he is unfit for duty after a strange incident X20 has engineered. But when X20 turns his evil attentions on Troy, he is thwarted and Phones revealed to be alright all along.

## 26. INVISIBLE ENEMY

*Script by Alan Fennell*
*Directed by David Elliott*

A man in a trance, found by Troy, is left at Marineville.  But the man is under hypnotic orders from an underwater race to similarly entrance all  at Marineville. With Marina's help, Troy saves everyone, including the innocent stranger.

## 27. DEEP HEAT

*Script by  Alan Fennell*
*Directed by John Kelly*

Two underwater beings lure Stingray to the bottom of the ocean and then steal

Troy and Phones' breathing equipment. But Marina refuses to let them into Stingray, and Troy and Phones regain control of the situation.

## 28. IN SEARCH OF THE TAJMANON

*Script by  Dennis Spooner*
*Directed by Desmond Saunders*

A palace that was submerged underwater has now disappeared.  When Stingray aids a Professor looking for a missing palace, they end up in Africa, where the Palace has been transported and re-built, brick by brick.

## 29. TITAN GOES POP

*Script by Alan Fennell*
*Directed by  Alan Pattillo*

After noticing a disruption caused to Marineville's daily life, Titan and X20 abduct the man responsible - a famous pop singer.  After questioning him, X20 returns him safely to the surface, glad of the "sabotage" performed by this man who can so easily disturb the normal Marineville routine.

## 30. SET SAIL FOR ADVENTURE

*Script by  Dennis Spooner*
*Directed by David Elliott*

While captaining an old sailing ship, Commander Shore's friend Admiral Denver is concussed in a storm and loses his memory.  After casting two men adrift and firing on Stingray, he is overcome by Troy.  Denver is again knocked out, and when he awakes, has forgotten all that happened.

## 31. TUNE OF DANGER

*Script by Alan Fennell*
*Directed by John Kelly*

The WASP jazz group is sabotaged by an underwater spy who places a bomb in an instrument. Troy discovers this plot and must win a race against time to save his friends.

## 32. RESCUE FROM THE SKIES

*Script by Dennis Spooner*
*Directed by Desmond Saunders*

X20 is able to place a sticker bomb on Stingray while Troy is away. Troy must

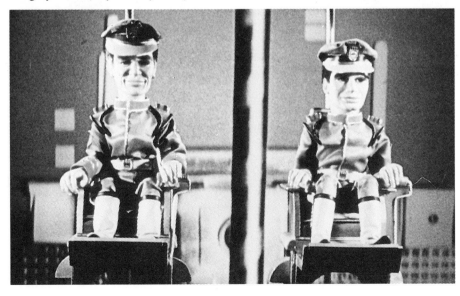

be parachuted in. In one of the most difficult tasks of his career, Troy removes the bomb without it exploding.

## 33. THE COOL CAVEMAN

*Script by Alan Fennell*
*Directed by Alan Pattillo*

Atlanta is giving a fancy dress party and, wondering what to wear, Troy falls asleep. He dreams of saving some underwater cavemen from radio-activity. Awakening, the dream inspires him, but when he arrives at the party he discovers everyone has had the idea of dressing as cavemen.

## 34. A NUT FOR MARINEVILLE

*Script by Gerry and Sylvia Anderson*
*Directed by David Elliott*

Professor Burgoyne is bought in when Stingray's missiles fail to damage an enemy ship. After some anxious moments, the Professor creates a new missile which destroys the enemy craft and saves Marineville.

## 35. TRAPPED IN THE DEPTHS

*Script by Alan Fennell*
*Directed By John Kelly*

Troy, Phones and Atlanta are trapped at a remote underwater station when Stingray is stolen by underwater people who plan to attack Marineville. The thieves are slaves of an unbalanced surface man, and Troy forces him to recall Stingray, ending his plot.

## 36. EASTERN ECLIPSE

*Script by Alan Fennell*
*Directed by Desmond Saunders*

X20 attempts to swap the imprisoned El Hudat (see Episode 24) for his identical twin brother. But when the plan goes wrong and the brothers end up in the sea, both must be locked up as they are dressed identically.

## 37. A CHRISTMAS TO REMEMBER

*Script by Dennis Spooner*
*Directed by Alan Pattillo*

When Troy takes an orphan aboard
Stingray to celebrate Christmas, the boy
gets unexpected excitement. Phones is
captured by an enemy and the boy looks
on as Troy saves the day.

## 38. THE LIGHTHOUSE DWELLERS

*Script by Alan Fennell*
*Directed by David Elliott*

A lighthouse closed because it is
dangerous, begins to operate again.
Troy discovers that the light has been
keeping an underwater civilisation alive.
He finds a solution that provides the
power the civilisation needs without
endangering men.

## 39. AQUANAUT OF THE YEAR

*Script by Gerry and Sylvia Anderson*
*Directed by Alan Pattillo*

After winning the 'Aquanaut of the Year'
Award, Troy appears on 'This Is Your
Life', where many of his adventures with
World Aquanaut Security Patrol are re-
capped, and the depth of his friendship
with Atlanta is explored.

### Voices
Commander Shore...Ray Barrett
Troy Tempest...Don Mason
'Phones' Sheridan...Robert Easton
Atlanta Shore...Lois Maxwell
Titan...Ray Barrett
Agent X 2 Zero...Robert Easton

### Principal Credits

39 thirty minute episodes
Colour
Producer : Gerry Anderson
Director of Photography : John Read
Special Effects : Derek Meddings and
Reg Hill
Music Composer, Arranger and
Conductor : Barry Gray
Art Director : Bob Bell
Puppetry Supervision :
Christine Glanville and Mary Turner
Character Visualisation :
Sylvia Anderson

1965

**International Rescue**- a secret organisation with headquarters based somewhere in the Pacific, always on the look-out for trouble, alert to help the rest of humanity in the year 2063. Dynamically overseen by intrepid astronaut, Jeff Tracy, and staffed by his five sons, the main power of this fighting force is its five super-secret craft... the Thunderbirds!

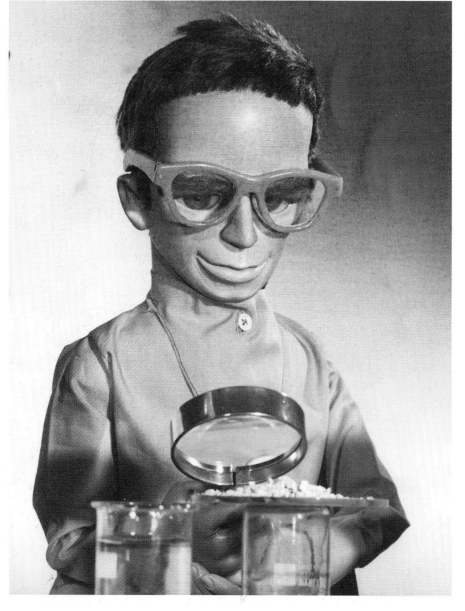

## Characters

JEFF TRACY - the resolute astronaut who founded the International Rescue Organisation and co-ordinates it from his secret base, Tracy Island
SCOTT TRACY - Jeff's eldest son, versatile pilot of Thunderbird 1. Responsible for assessing trouble and directing operations on the spot.
VIRGIL TRACY - the staunch, reliable pilot of Thunderbird 2.
ALAN TRACY - impetuous and lady-killing, he pilots Thunderbird 3.
GORDON TRACY - Virgil's jocular co-pilot, who also mans Thunderbird 4 when needed.

  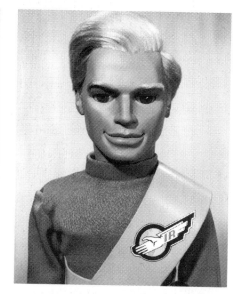

JOHN TRACY - responsible for the essential duty of manning space monitor Thunderbird 5.

BRAINS - the shy scientific wiz who invented the Thunderbirds and is constantly coming up with new ideas for gadgets and machines.

LADY PENELOPE - International Rescue's elegant, glamorous London agent who is driven around in her shocking-pink Rolls Royce, licence plate FAB 1, by....

PARKER- Lady Penelope's chauffeur, a Cockney ex-criminal with plenty of useful (though occasionally illegal) skills.

THE HOOD - a tyrannical villain with mysterious hypnotic powers and a determination to undermine International Rescue and learn the secrets of the Thunderbirds craft.

KYRANO - Jeff Tracy's loyal servant, over whom the Hood (his evil half brother) has a strange hypnotic power and influence...

TIN-TIN - Kyrano's daughter, an electronics expert who works closely with Brains with a definite fondness for Alan Tracy.

GRANDMA - Jeff Tracy's mother, who just loves cooking and looking after her grandsons.

*Thunderbird 1* - the fastest flying machine on Earth, at 7000 miles an hour always first on the spot!

*Thunderbird 2* - the chunky cargo vehicle, fitted with pods to carry any necessary bulky equipment to the site of a rescue, including:

*The Mole* - a drilling machine for the rescue of those trapped underground. Carried to the scene aboard Thunderbird 2, it then moves along the ground on caterpillar tracks; and

*The Thunderizer* - a blasting cannon with a cutting laser beam used to get rid of obstacles and cut through metal.

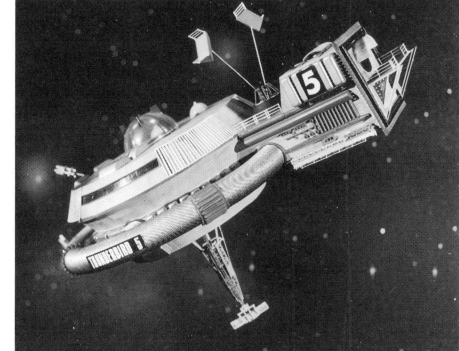

*Thunderbird 3* - a rocket capable of flying into space. Used for transport to Thunderbird 5 and space rescue.
*Thunderbird 4* - the underwater scout craft carried to and from trouble zones aboard Thunderbird 2.
*Thunderbird 5* - the super satellite orbiting the Earth that monitors communications around the globe, listening for calls for help!
*FAB 1* - Lady Penelope's distinctive pink Rolls Royce, equipped with grappling hooks and machine guns.
*FAB 2* - Lady Penelope's rather more conventional yacht.

## 1. TRAPPED IN THE SKY
*Directed by Alan Pattillo*
*Script by Gerry and Sylvia Anderson*

The Hood places a bomb aboard an airliner in order to be able to photograph the Thunderbirds craft as they attempt to rescue it. International Rescue must simultaneously save Tin-Tin, who is aboard the airliner, and thwart the Hood's devious plans.

## 2. PIT OF PERIL
*Directed by Desmond Saunders*
*Script by Alan Fennell*

When a revolutionary new Army transport vehicle 'The Sidewinder' is tested, it runs into trouble and disappears beneath the ground. International Rescue is called, and with mens' lives at stake, a highly ingenious and dangerous operation devised by Brains must be executed perfectly to succeed.

## 3. CITY OF FIRE
*Directed by David Elliott*
*Script by Alan Fennell*

A terrifying fire breaks out in a vast

shopping mart. Everyone is evacuated except for a single family who are trapped in a sealed-off corridor. Against overwhelming odds, Scott and Virgil save the family before the whole area explodes.

## 4. SUN PROBE
*Directed by Alan Pattillo*
*Script by Alan Fennell*

A research space ship loses its direction and is on a collision course with the sun. Using some of Brains' latest equipment, Alan and Scott in Thunderbird 3 save

the probe ship and narrowly avoid crashing into the sun themselves.

## 5. THE UNINVITED
*Directed by Desmond Saunders*
*Script by Alan Fennell*

Scott is forced down in the desert by three mysterious jet fighters with weird, unfamiliar markings. He and two archaeologists are captured by his attackers, the Zombites, a lost race living in a huge pyramid. Scott manages to create blind confusion in the Zombites' headquarters, the three escape and the pyramid is destroyed.

## 6. THE MIGHTY ATOM
*Directed by David Lane*
*Script by Dennis Spooner*

The Hood audaciously steals 'The Mighty Atom', a robot rat that can be programmed to take photographs. He plans to photograph the Thunderbirds, but fortunately for International Rescue, during its mission the Mighty Atom stumbles on another subject. When the Hood retrieves the film all he finds is shots of Lady Penelope - screaming her head off at the life-like rat!

## 7. VAULT OF DEATH

*Directed by David Elliott*
*Script by Dennis Spooner*

At the Bank of England, an employee has been trapped in a time-lock vault that is set to remain closed for two years. The air is being pumped out and the employee will soon die. Thunderbirds arrive to save the man and begin to burn their way in. With time running out the situation is desperate - until Penelope and Parker arrives and he opens the vault with one of her hairpins!

## 8. OPERATION CRASH DIVE

*Directed by Desmond Saunders*
*Script by Martin Clump*

Two giant Fireflash airliners have crashed into the Atlantic under mysterious circumstances. Although

International Rescue manage to save the pilot of the second crash, they can find no explanation for it. On a third flight, Thunderbird 2 follows the Fireflash, and the cause of the trouble is located - a saboteur hidden in the wing. At the last moment, Gordon repairs the sabotage and the Fireflash is saved.

## 9. MOVE AND YOU'RE DEAD

*Directed by Alan Pattillo*
*Script by Alan Pattillo*

A jealous racing driver strands Alan Tracy and Grandma on a new road bridge with an ultra-sonic device connected to a bomb so that if they move, they die. But Brains ingeniously disables the bomb from long-distance. The two are saved, and it is left up to Scott to track down the driver who has stolen Alan's prize-winning car.

## 10. MARTIAN INVASION

*Directed by David Elliott*
*Script by Alan Fennell*

Using his half-brother Kyrano, the Hood immobilizes the photodetector in Thunderbird 1. Thus when Scott goes to the rescue of two actors trapped during filming of a Martian invasion movie, the Hood is able to photograph the craft. But he is discovered, and in his attempts to deliver the film to his customer, General Strond, it is destroyed.

## 11. BRINK OF DISASTER

*Directed by David Lane*
*Script by Alan Fennell*

When Jeff Tracy, Brains and Tin-Tin are taken on a monorail journey by Warren Grafton, it almost ends in disaster. The track has been negligently built by Grafton's crooked outfit and it takes the full resources of Brains and Thunderbirds 1 and 2 to save the four passengers. Then Grafton and the other crooks are made safe - behind bars.

## 12. THE PERILS OF PENELOPE

*Directed by Alan Pattillo and*
*Desmond Saunders*
*Script by Alan Pattillo*

Investigating the disappearance of an accomplished scientist, Lady Penelope is similarly kidnapped. In an attempt to force the scientist to reveal his secrets, Penelope is tied directly in the path of an oncoming express train. Will he talk? But such questions are irrelevant as Virgil and Gordon save Penelope - just as the express train rushes into view.

## 13. TERROR IN NEW YORK

*Directed by David Lane and
David Elliott
Script by Alan Fennell*

Disaster strikes when the Empire State
Building is moved to a new site to allow
development of the old one. A TV
reporter and cameraman are trapped in a
cave-in. Brains surmises that they can
be reached from an underground
network of streams, but as Gordon
rushes to meet the two men in
Thunderbird 4, another building
collapses. The two men are saved, just
before a gigantic tidal wave sweeps
through behind them.

## 14. END OF THE ROAD

*Directed David Lane
Script by Dennis Spooner*

There is a double problem when a man
who knows the Tracy family is in
extreme danger. After a dangerous
demolition operation, Eddie Houseman
is helplessly stranded in his tractor on
the brink of a cliff. He must be saved -
but without learning that International

Rescue comprises his friends, the
Tracys. Scott and Virgil keep their
identities secure by staying within their
vehicles and hauling Eddie to safety.

## 15. A DAY OF DISASTER

*Directed by David Elliott
Script by Dennis Spooner*

A Martian probe-rocket collapses with
two engineers in its nose cone. And
then the countdown begins...
International Rescue must save the two
men before the rocket is destructively
launched - but it is buried beneath tons
of rubble. For hours they work until the
nose cone is finally detached and the
engineers freed, just before the rocket
fires and disintegrates against a river
bank.

## 16. THE EDGE OF IMPACT

*Directed by Desmond Saunders
Script by Donald Robertson*

Two men are endangered when an
aircraft sabotaged by the Hood crashes
into their Telerelay Station. The Control
Room at the top is swaying in the wind

and will soon collapse. They cannot be
rescued directly, but a capsule fired from
Thunderbird 2 contains escape harnesses
for the men, and when the structure
finally falls the two are saved.

## 17. DESPERATE INTRUDER

*Directed by David Lane
Script by Donald Robertson*

Brains and Tin-Tin are on a search for
golden treasure. They don aquasuits to
dive into a lake where the treasure may
be.... the Hood lays in wait then uses his
hypnotic powers on the hunters ....... but
buried to his neck in sand, Brains still
refuses to reveal the lake's location .....
the Hood attacks again..... in the battle
his craft is destroyed, the treasure lost,
and Brains trapped...... Finally, Brains is
saved and order restored.

## 18. 30 MINUTES BEFORE NOON

*Directed by David Elliott
Script by Alan Fennell*

When a mission to undermine a
complex sabotage operation goes wrong,
a British agent is left with a bomb in a
bracelet clamped to his arm, trapped
under robot guard in a well-shielded
plutonium storage room. The world's
biggest explosion will happen at 12.30.
Unless.... International Rescue are
forced to succeed at a highly delicate
operation that involves breaching the
plutonium security zone and disposing
of the explosive bracelet.

## 22. DANGER AT OCEAN DEEP

*Directed by Desmond Saunders*
*Script by Donald Robertson*

One ship, Ocean Pioneer 1, has disappeared. And just after Ocean Pioneer is launched, Brains discovers that its cargo of liquid alsterene destines it for disaster too. Even with a mysterious communications blackout hindering them, Thunderbirds locate the ship. Amid growing radiation, the crew is finally saved, but the vessel explodes.

## 23. THE DUCHESS ASSIGNMENT

*Directed by David Elliott*
*Script by Martin Crump*

Lady Penelope's friend, the elderly Duchess of Royston, arranges to loan a valuable painting to an American businessman. En route to deliver the painting, she is kidnapped by two crooks - but notifies International Rescue with a concealed homing device Penelope has given her. The crooks are caught and the Duchess rescued from the burning building she has been imprisoned in.

## 24. ATTACK OF THE ALLIGATORS

*Directed by David Lane*
*Script by Alan Patillo*

After accidently pouring a quantity of enlarging drug into a swamp river, four

men are trapped in their house by giant alligators. Alan, Virgil and Gordon manage to put the four beasts out of action, but subsequently a whole phial full of enlarging liquid, drops in the river. Gordon swims to search for it, and finally recovers the phial - mercifully intact.

## 19. THE IMPOSTERS

*Directed by Desmond Saunders*
*Script by Dennis Spooner*

Two men posing as International Rescue agents save a man trapped in a well and steal secret papers from an adjacent underground vault. With their reputation sullied, International Rescue's freedom to operate is curtailed and there is a man in dire trouble in space. Suddenly, Penelope comes through with the imposters' identity, and Alan and Scott can at last rescue the drifting spaceman.

## 20. THE MAN FROM M.I.5

*Directed by David Lane*
*Script by Alan Fennell*

While investigating the disappearance of British secret agent Bondson and some

terrible dangerous nuclear plans, Lady Penelope is kidnapped and left with a remote-controlled bomb. But the kidnappers have not reckoned with the radio built into Penelope's powder compact! The Thunderbirds are alerted, the murderers are trapped, Lady Penelope is saved.... and the plans are regained.

## 21. CRY WOLF

*Directed by David Elliott*
*Script by Dennis Spooner*

After two Australian boys have raised a false alarm, their second call for help is at first ignored. But when American satellite HQ confirms that the boys' father (one of the operatives) is under assault from the Hood, Thunderbirds rush to the rescue. The pursued Hood tumbles over a cliff, and the two small boys are saved.

## 25. THE CHAM CHAM

*Directed by Alan Pattillo*
*Script by Alan Pattillo*

Musical arranger Olsen has been using the live broadcasts of a famous pop group to sabotage American rocket transporter flights with a sensitive ultrasonic device, the Cham Cham. Posing as a singer, Penelope interrupts the next broadcast, and using exactly the right key and tempo, sings the transporter to safety. Olsen is captured by Virgil and Alan in Thunderbird 2.

## 26. SECURITY HAZARD

*Directed by Desmond Saunders*
*Script by Alan Pattillo*

Chip, a small boy, stows away and manages to reach Tracy Island. When Jeff discovers him learning International Rescue secrets, he decides the boy is a security hazard that must be neutralized. When Chip falls asleep he is whisked home to his own bed, and is left believing the whole escapade was a dream.

## 27. ALANTIC INFERNO

*Directed by Desmond Saunders*
*Script by Alan Fennell*

While Jeff is on holiday, Scott is left in charge on International Rescue. He

successfully masterminds an operation to save all the occupants of a stricken oil rig that is slowly destroyed by fire. But by the time Jeff returns, it has been too much for Scott - now he needs a holiday!

## 28. PATH OF DESTRUCTION

*Directed by David Elliott*
*Script by Donald Robertson*

The massive, atomic powered 'Crablogger' that cuts down and processes trees into pulp goes out of control and razes a town to the ground. Virgil and Scott risk death to shut down its reactor and empty its fuel tanks before it destroys a local dam.

## 29. ALIAS MR. HACKENBACKER

*Directed by Desmond Saunders*
*Script by Alan Pattillo*

Crooks try to hijack a plane on which Lady Penelope is hosting a fashion show. She contacts Thunderbirds who force the plane to make a crash landing. But all aboard are saved as the plane has been fitted with a safety device invented by Brains - under his alias 'Mr. Hackenbacker'. The frustrated crooks are captured and led away.

## 30. LORD PARKER'S 'OLIDAY

*Directed by Brian Burgess*
*Script by Tony Barwick*

Lady Penelope and Parker holiday at the first town to be lit by solar power. But during their first night there a giant reflector used to concentrate the sun's rays crashes. As the sun rises, the Thunderbirds must race against time to prevent the town being destroyed by the magnified heat.

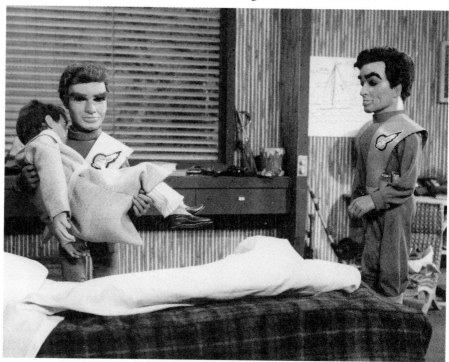

## 31. RICOCHET

*Directed by Brian Burgess*
*Script by Tony Barwick*

In space, a pirate TV station is damaged by the destruction of a faulty rocket and is destined for burn-out on re-entry of the atmosphere. Thunderbird 5 is malfunctioning and cannot help. Tin-Tin picks up an SOS TV message from the pirates, and Thunderbirds 2 and 3 save the crew - but their unauthorised spacecraft blows up in the desert.

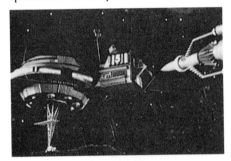

## 32. GIVE OR TAKE A MILLION

*Directed by Desmond Saunders*
*Script by Alan Pattillo*

When two bank robbers trip an alarm, they try to hide but are transported along with a consignment of hundreds of gifts to a childrens' hospital. The crooks are captured and one lucky child gets the Christmas of a lifetime at Tracy Island.

### Principal Credits

32 sixty minute episodes
Colour
An AP Films Production in association with ATV for ITC World-wide Distribution
Series created by:
Gerry and Sylvia Anderson
Executive Producer : Gerry Anderson
Producer : Reg Hill
Director of Photography : John Read
Music and Electronic Effects :
Barry Gray
Series Created by
Gerry and Sylvia Anderson
Art Director : Bob Bell
Special Effects Supervisor :
Derek Meddings
Puppetry Supervision : Mary Turner
Character Visualisation :
Sylvia Anderson

### Voices

| | |
|---|---|
| Jeff Tracy...Peter Dyneley | Brains...David Graham |
| Scott Tracy...Shane Rimmer | Parker...David Graham |
| Virgil Tracy...David Holliday | Kyrano...David Graham |
| Alan Tracy...Matt Zimmerman | Tin-Tin...Christine Finn |
| Gordon Tracy...David Graham | Grandma...Christine Finn |
| John Tracy...Ray Barrett | Lady Penelope...Sylvia Anderson |
| | The Hood...Ray Barrett |

1967

After a landing on Mars made in the year 2065 by Spectrum, Earth's security organisation, the Mysterons from Mars mistakenly believe that Earth has launched an unprovoked attack on them and their planet. They retaliate and, in the process, two Spectrum agents - Captain Scarlet and Captain Black - gain the power to re-create themselves, even after being killed. Scarlet maintains his loyalty and his position as Spectrum's best agent, but Captain Black becomes the Mysterons' pawn in the war which they begin to wage against Earth!

## Characters

**CAPTAIN SCARLET** (Paul Metcalfe) - Spectrum's number one, indestructible, agent. Six hours under the control of the Mysterons has given him the power of retrometabolism.

**COLONEL WHITE** (Charles Grey) - the dedicated Commander in Chief of Spectrum Cloudbase. In charge of all Spectrum personnel both on Cloudbase and on Earth.

**CAPTAIN BLUE** (Adam Svenson) - a brilliant, fearless pilot and member of Spectrum. Usually works together with Captain Scarlet.

**CAPTAIN GREY** (Bradley Holden) - one of Spectrum's most reliable agents, previously Security Commander of the World Aquanaut Security Patrol.

**LIEUTENANT GREEN** (Seymour Griffiths) - Colonel White's right hand man in the Cloudbase Control Room. He operates the computer which is the heart of Spectrum's communications and information systems.

**CAPTAIN OCHRE** (Richard Frazer) - member of Spectrum. Previously led a squad in the World Government Police Corps.

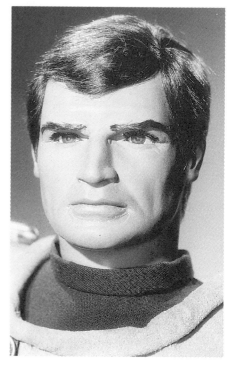

CAPTAIN MAGENTA (Patrick Donaghue) - member of Spectrum. Previously ran a criminal syndicate in New York and has immense knowledge of crime and the underworld.

DOCTOR FAWN (Edward Wilkie) - the resident Spectrum doctor at Cloudbase.

**Voices**

Captain Scarlet....Francis Matthews
Colonel White, Captain Black and The Voice of the Mysterons....Donald Gray
Captain Grey and World President.. Paul Maxwell
Captain Blue....Ed Bishop
Captain Ochre and Supporting characters...Jeremy Wilkin
Captain Magenta....Gary Files
Lieutenant Green....Cy Grant
Doctor Fawn....Charles Tingwell
Melody Angel....Sylvia Anderson
Symphony Angel....Janna Hill
Rhapsody and Destiny Angels.... Liz Morgan
Harmony Angel....Lian-Shin

CAPTAIN BLACK - a Spectrum agent, leader of an expedition to Mars, who has been taken over by the Mysterons and turned into a Mysteron agent.

RHAPSODY ANGEL (DIANE SIMS) - a wealthy society girl who was a security officer with an airline before joining the Angels.

MELODY ANGEL (Magnolia Jones) - a member of the Angel team previously a brilliant pilot in the World Army Air Force.

SYMPHONY ANGEL (Karen

Wainwright) - member of the Angel team of pilots.

HARMONY ANGEL (Chan Kwan) - member of the Angel team of pilots, previously a record-breaking round the world flyer.

DESTINY ANGEL (Juliette Pontoin) - (leader) of the Spectrum Angels with a previous outstanding record in the World Army Air Force.

## THE MACHINES

Angel Aircraft - single-seater jet capable of top speed in excess of 3,000 mph. The main strike aircraft of Spectrum. Flown by the Angels, three are always on the aeriel launch platform on Cloudbase ready for take-off.

Spectrum Saloon - five-seater saloon car capable of speeds exceeding 150 mph. Tyres and windscreen are bullet-proof.

Spectrum Pursuit Vehicle - 25 ft long bullet-proof vehicle. Max. speed of over 200 mph. Has no windscreen - driver faces backwards and drives by

means of a TV monitor showing him the road ahead. SPV's are concealed in strategic positions all over the world.

Spectrum Helijet - general purpose helicopter used for transporting Spectrum personnel.

Spectrum Passenger Jet - seven-passenger jet used for transporting Spectrum personnel. Range of 12,000 miles.

Spectrum Maximum Security Vehicles - specifically designed for transporting V.I.P.'s in safety. Weighs 8 tons and has bullet-proof, practically indestructible shell.

## 1. THE MYSTERONS

*Script by Gerry Anderson*
*Directed by Desmond Saunders*

After misunderstanding the first Spectrum landing on Mars, the Mysterons declare war on Earth and take over Captain Black's mind. In a failed attempt by the Mysterons to assassinate the World President, Captain Scarlet is killed. But the Mysterons' previous failed attempts to control Scarlet have left him with the magic property that enables his body to re-create itself, and he comes alive again. Now Scarlet is an even greater asset to Spectrum in the war with the Mysterons.

## 2. WINGED ASSASSIN

*Script by Tony Barwick*
*Directed by David Lane*

Over the Atlantic a jet plane explodes and crashes into the sea. Seconds later, the plane re-appears, climbs steadily into the air... and the Mysteron 'M' slides over its outline. When Captain Scarlet, protecting the Director General of the United Asian Republic, is attacked by this plane, he faces his first big test. He must deliberately sacrifice his life and prove his invincibility to save the Director General.

## 3. BIG BEN STRIKES AGAIN

*Script by Tony Barwick*
*Directed by Brian Burgess*

The Mysterons announce that they will destroy London, and then a transporter with a nuclear device aboard is hijacked.

Captain Blue calculates the location of the transporter from information gleaned from a man who heard Big Ben chime thirteen times. It is then left to Scarlet to drive the transporter deep within the Earth, to an explosion only he could survive.

## 4. MANHUNT

*Script by Tony Barwick*
*Directed by Alan Perry*

When Captain Black breaches security and enters an atomic plant, Colonel White has his first definite proof of the Mysterons' control of Black. Black has exposed himself to radiation, and Scarlet participates in a manhunt with directional geiger counters. But Black manages to capture Symphony Angel. Though the voice of the Mysterons predicts her death in three minutes, Symphony is rescued unhurt. Black cleanses himself of radiation and escapes.

## 5. POINT 783

*Script by Peter Curran and*
*David Williams*
*Directed by Bob Lynn*

The Mysterons warn that they will destroy the Supreme Commander of Earth Forces. Then they kill and reconstruct two of the Supreme

Commander's aides. Captain Scarlet must frustrate the murder attempts of each of the two in turn, which he does - even in the face of the Unitron, a revolutionary new weapon.

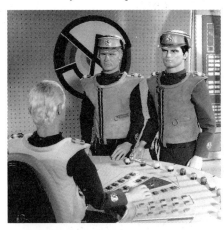

## 6. OPERATION TIME

*Script by Richard Conway and*
*Stephen Mattick*
*Directed by Ken Turner*

When the voice of the Mysterons threatens to "kill time", Spectrum must protect General Tiempo, whose name in Spanish means time. But when Tiempo undergoes an operation, the surgeon has been replaced by a Mysteron agent, and administers a lethal dose of power to the patient. But then it is revealed that the Mysterons have failed - Scarlet has taken the place of the General, who is safe elsewhere.

## 7. RENEGADE ROCKET

*Script by Ralph Hart*
*Directed by Brian Burgess*

A Major taken over by the Mysterons penetrates a top security rocket base, kills its controller, launches the rocket at an unknown destination and escapes. While the Angels hunt down the wayward Major, it is left to Scarlet to discover the target of the rocket - which turns out to be the secret rocket base itself - and with only thirty seconds to spare, make it self-destruct.

## 8. WHITE AS SNOW

*Script by Peter Curran and*
*David Williams*
*Directed by Robert Lynn*

In a drastic measure to save Colonel White, who has become the target for the Mysterons' next act of retaliation, Captain Scarlet must attack him. Back at Spectrum HQ, White sentences Scarlet to death for insubordination. But the order is soon cancelled - a firing squad would be useless against the indestructible Scarlet!

## 9. SEEK AND DESTROY

*Script by Peter Curran and*
*David Williams*
*Directed by Alan Perry*

In a plan to kill the Spectrum Angels, the Mysterons cause the destruction of 3 Angel aircraft. Reconstructed as Mysteron aircraft, they first attack Destiny, and then precipitate a dogfight with Melody, Rhapsody and Harmony Angels. In the ensuing combat, Harmony is forced to eject - but all three Mysteron craft are destroyed.

## 10. SPECTRUM STRIKES BACK

*Script by Tony Barwick*
*Directed by Ken Turner*

Captain Scarlet attends a secret conference in a concealed lodge where two new weapons in the war against the Mysterons are unveiled: the Mysteron Gun and the Mysteron Detector. Captain Black's attempt to infiltrate the conference with a man he has killed and reconstructed is foiled by the use of these new weapons.

## 11. AVALANCHE

*Script by Shane Rimmer*
*Directed by Brian Burgess*

The Mysterons attempt to destroy the string of bases that make up the Outer Space Defence System. They "take over" a trusted truck driver who begins to destroy bases one by one. But when Scarlet discovers the method of sabotage, he chases the truck driver who is finally buried in an avalanche.

## 12. THE SHADOW OF FEAR

*Script by Tony Barwick*
*Directed by Bob Lynn*

In a clever operation, a satellite is concealed on one of Mars' moons to take photos of the Mysterons' secret base and beam the pictures back to Earth. But by the time the transmission station has become operative, with Scarlet waiting to see first pictures, the Mysterons have retaliated and caused the destruction of the receiving station on Earth. Spectrum's plan is foiled.

## 13. THE TRAP

*Script by Alan Pattillo*
*Directed by Alan Perry*

In trying to prevent the Mysterons' attempt to wipe out the entire World Air Force Supreme Command, Captain Scarlet is trapped in a dungeon. He escapes to save the Supreme Command from being machine-gunned, but the Mysterons have a second chance, and Scarlet must distract another machine-gunner while Symphony Angel flies the Supreme Command to safety.

## 14. SPECIAL ASSIGNMENT

*Script by Tony Barwick*
*Directed by Bob Lynn*

Captain Scarlet gambles all his money away, resigns Spectrum, steals an S.P.V.,

agrees to provide Captain Black with a nuclear device which he will use to blow up Nuclear City and start a chain reaction that would destroy North America, and shoots Captain Blue. Can it be true? No! Scarlet is merely operating undercover for Spectrum to thwart the Mysterons' latest plan.

## 15. LUNARVILLE 7

*Script by Tony Barwick*
*Directed by Bob Lynn*

It seems that the Lunar Control of Man's largest settlement on the Moon, Lunarville 7, has negotiated itself a neutrality with the Mysterons. But when Spectrum's men travel to the moon to check the reports, the Lunar Controller frustrates Scarlet at every turn. Scarlet discovers an unauthorized Mysteron complex under construction and, in the ensuing confrontation, the Lunar Controller causes the destruction of the whole Lunarville Complex.

## 16. HEART OF NEW YORK

*Script by Tony Barwick*
*Directed by Alan Perry*

When Mysterons threaten to destroy the centre of New York, it is evacuated. But

when three robbers break into the 2nd National Bank, in the now-empty centre of New York, they are discovered by Captain Black, and they cancel out each other's evil plans. The bank's vault is not breached, Captain Black is chased away by Captains Scarlet and Blue, and New York is saved.

## 17. THE TRAITOR

*Script by Tony Barwick*
*Directed by Alan Perry*

After the Mysterons broadcast that Spectrum will be sabotaged from within, a series of hovercraft accidents cast suspicion on Captain Scarlet. In a training exercise, another hovercraft begins to falter. But Scarlet orders all other personnel to jump from the escape hatch of the hovercraft and stays to retrieve the black box instrument recorder. He escapes in the nick of time and with the black box demonstrates the true "traitor"... a tiny valve.

## 18. MODEL SPY

*Script by Bill Hedley*
*Directed by Ken Turner*

When the Mysterons threaten to kill a famous fashion designer, Captain Scarlet acts as the designer's Press Relations man. When two of the designer's models (who have been killed and reconstructed by the Mysterons) attempt to kill the designer, Scarlet, Blue, and Symphony and Destiny Angel save him - and he is so happy he presents the Angels with his latest fashionable creations.

## 19. FIRE AT RIG 15

*Script by Bryan Cooper*
*Directed by Ken Turner*

A disastrous fire at an oil rig in the Middle East leaves the Mysterons in control of an explosives expert. He is ordered by Captain Black to destroy the source of Spectrum's oil supplies, and in stopping him Scarlet narrowly avoids a catastrophe with a vulnerable pipe line.

## 20. FLIGHT TO ATLANTICA

*Script by Tony Barwick*
*Directed by Leo Eaton*

After Captains Blue and Ochre drink some drugged champagne that cause spasmodic amnesia and general irresponsibility, they begin to attack and destroy the World Navy Complex at Atlantica. Though Scarlet manages to stop them, they have already destroyed part of the complex, and the Mysterons have achieved a partial success.

## 21. CRATER 101

*Script by Tony Barwick*
*Directed by Ken Turner*

A dangerous mission to destroy a Mysteron complex on the moon becomes deadly for Captains Scarlet and Blue and Lieutenant Green when the detonator on their nuclear weapon is set

forward by their enemy. Fast action is required when they suddenly discover that they don't have two hours to evacuate the area - but just one minute!

## 22. DANGEROUS RENDEZVOUS

*Script by Tony Barwick*
*Directed by Brian Burgess*

A "diamond pulsator" Captain Scarlet has recovered from the Moon is used to make direct contact with the Mysterons on Mars. Colonel White attempts to negotiate an end to the war of nerves with them, but the Mysterons' response is treachery. After a series of escapes from Mysteron attacks, Scarlet must act quickly to stop the "diamond pulsator" itself from destroying Cloudbase.

## 23. NOOSE OF ICE

*Script by Peter Curran and Derek Williams*
*Directed by Ken Turner*

The Mysterons threaten to destroy the New World Space Fleet. The scene of their attack will be a Tritonium mine at the North Pole. But when Scarlet arrives there, he is unaware the attack has already begun. The mining station's

main power line is cut and Scarlet has little time to discover the culprit and reconnect the power to avert the threat of the entire station being frozen and destroyed by ice.

## 24. TREBLE CROSS

*Script by Tony Barwick*
*Directed by Alan Perry*

When a Major of the World Air Force is forced off the road by Captain Black, he is reconstructed by the Mysterons, as part of a plan to destroy the World Capital. But the major's body is discovered and when revived, his heart begins to beat again, and the Mysteron reconstruction of him is revealed. It is up to Scarlet to reverse the deception and fool Captain Black, saving the World Capital.

90

## 25. INFERNO

*Script by Shane Rimmer and*
*Tony Barwick*
*Directed by Alan Perry*

When the Mysterons threaten to destroy a vital water facility in South America, Captains Ochre, Magenta, Scarlet and Blue are sent to protect it.  But despite this, and with Captain Black's assistance, the Mysterons score a victory with their devious plan, by homing a reconstructed spacecraft in on their Earthly target.

## 26. FLIGHT 104

*Script by Tony Barwick*
*Directed by Bob Lynn*

The Mysterons plan to sabotage a conference which Dr Conrad, a leading astro-physicist, is to attend.  Captains Scarlet and Blue are assigned to protect him, but on their first plane flight, the pilots are done away with, and Scarlet and Blue must take the controls.  But an electrical problem develops, and the only solution is for Scarlet to crash-land the plane - and take the consequences!

## 27. PLACE OF THE ANGELS

*Script by Leo Eaton*
*Directed by Leo Eaton*

Spectrum is mystified by the Mysterons' latest threat - to destroy 'The Place of the Angels'.  But when a deadly plague culture is stolen, Captains Scarlet and Blue and the Angels trace its thief to Los Angeles - the Place of the Angels! The thief is about to drop the plague culture into the city's water supply, and Scarlet must make a tremendous effort to prevent this catastrophe, and stop the drop with only seconds to spare.

## 28. EXPO 2068

*Script by Shane Rimmer*
*Directed by Leo Eaton*

The Mysterons destroy and reconstruct a revolutionary nuclear reactor and its transporting lorry.  It is driven to the site of Expo 2068 and a safety valve removed.  Though Spectrum detects the sabotaged reactor, it is now overheating and may set off a nuclear explosion.  It is up to Scarlet to deactivate the reactor in time and thwart the Mysterons.

## 29.  THE LAUNCHING

*Script by Peter Curran and*
*David Williams*
*Directed by Brian Burgess*

President Roberts must be protected for the Mysterons have threatened his life. The launch of a new atomic liner named after Roberts is the site of the planned assassination and Scarlet must prevent several ingenious attempts by a newsman who has been killed and converted to the Mysterons' evil ways.

## 30. CODENAME EUROPA

*Script by David Lee*
*Directed by Alan Perry*

An electronics wizard is killed and reconstructed by the Mysterons, who plan to use his technical know-how to kill the three joint presidents of the Congress of Europe.  Spectrum foils his attempt to  kill the first president, and when he moves on to attack the second, Scarlet is there and overcomes the electronics genius with a simple trap - a wire in his path which trips him up!

## 31. ATTACK ON CLOUDBASE

*Script by Tony Barwick*
*Directed by Ken Turner*

Symphony Angel's aircraft explodes and she is forced to eject into the parched and barren desert. As she collapses, delirious from the heat, she hears a Mysteron threat to destroy Cloudbase. The situation gets worse; Cloudbase is moved to a remote area; Scarlet is killed outright; and then Cloudbase receives a direct hit. There's no hope for Cloudbase - except that Symphony awakens and realises it has all been a dream!

## 32. THE INQUISITION

*Script by Tony Barwick*
*Directed by Ken Turner*

Captain Blue is drugged and when he wakes up he is told that three months have passed. He is questioned aboard Cloudbase by a man claiming to be from Spectrum Intelligence, and told he must reveal secret cipher codes to prove his identity. But when he refuses and tries to escape, his way is blocked. He jumps from the Cloudbase window, only to discover it is a mock-up. Captain Scarlet soon arrives to destroy the fake Cloudbase and rescue Captain Blue.

### Principal Credits

32 thirty minute episodes
Colour
A Century 21 Production in association with ATV for ITC World-Wide Distribution
Series created by

Gerry and Sylvia Anderson
Executive Producer: Gerry Anderson
Producer : Reg Hill
Supervising Director:
Desmond Saunders
Special Effects Supervisor: Derek Meddings

Script Editor: Tony Barwick
Music and Electronic Effects:
Barry Gray
Supervising Art Director: Bob Bell
Puppetry Co-ordinator: Mary Turner
Puppetry Supervision: Christine Glanville

1968

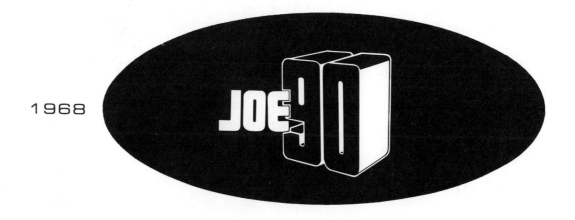

Brilliant electronics engineer Professor McClaine invents BIG RAT (Brian Impulse Galvanascope Record and Transfer), a machine that can record the brain patterns of one person and transfer them to another. Shane Weston, chief of the World Intelligence Network (an organisation based in America whose aim is to maintain the balance of power throughout the world), suggests that the machine be used to establish a new sort of secret agent. An agent with the power of BIG RAT behind him could draw on the skill and experience of any living person. Weston suggests the Professor's nine-year-old adopted son Joe for the job, because he could get into places that no grown-up could, and get out of sticky situations more easily, as a young boy would never be held responsible for any misdeeds. When Joe agrees to this, so is born Joe 90!

Joe has a special school case in which is hidden the WIN equipment he needs for his missions. One half contains his usual school kit but secret catches open to reveal his WIN badge and code book, transceiver, report book and automatic pistol as well as his BIG RAT adapted glasses which activate the brain patterns he has been given while sitting in the BIG RAT cage in his father's hidden laboratory.

## Characters

JOE 90 - Joe McClaine, the adopted son of Prof McLaine and WIN's top agent.
PROFESSOR IAN McCLAINE - Joe's guardian,' Mac', the electronics expert who is the inventor of BIG RAT.
SHANE WESTON - the Deputy Director of the World Intelligence Network and head of the London office.
SAM LOOVER - the deputy head of WIN's London office, and Joe 90's usual contact.
MRS ADA HARRIS - the McClaine's housekeeper, unaware of their secret.

| Voices | | |
|---|---|---|
| Joe 90 | .... | Len Jones |
| Mac | .... | Rupert Davies |
| Shane Weston | .... | David Healy |
| Sam Loover | .... | Keith Alexander |
| Mrs Harris | .... | Sylvia Anderson |

## 1. THE MOST SPECIAL AGENT

*Screenplay by*
*Gerry and Sylvia Anderson*
*Directed by Desmond Saunders*

After Professor McClaine shows his
new invention, BIG RAT, to Shane
Weston of WIN, the two decide to use
the machine to steal the latest Russian
plane. With the pre-recorded brain
patterns of a Russian pilot, Joe, the
Professor's son, is able to successfully
steal the plane and bring it back to
England. Joe has proven that with the
aid of BIG RAT, he has enormous
potential as WIN's most special agent.

## 2. HI-JACKED

*Screenplay by Tony Barwick*
*Directed by Alan Perry*

Following the murder of a WIN agent
investigating a ruthless gun-runner, Joe
is given the brain patterns of a top WIN
agent and stows away to get to the gun-
runner's hide-out. But he is discovered
and locked in the boot of a car that is to
be driven over the edge of a cliff.
However, with his pocket transmitter
and the aid of Sam Loover and his
father, Joe is able to outwit the gun-
runner.

## 3. SPLASH DOWN

*Screenplay by Shane Rimmer*
*Directed by Leo Eaton*

On two occasions the disappearance of
an electronics expert has been followed

by a major air crash. So WIN plans a
trap in which Professor McClaine, as a
world electronics expert, is the bait.
Sure enough, when he goes aboard a
plane with Joe, he is parachuted out of
the plane by captors and the pilot and
co-pilot are drugged. But with the brain
patterns of an air force pilot, Joe is able
to take over the plane, and with some
spectacular flying saves Mac and ends
the sinister plot.

## 4. INTERNATIONAL CONCERTO

*Screenplay by Tony Barwick*
*Directed by Alan Perry*

One of WIN's top agents is also a
world-famous concert pianist. But
while playing in an Eastern European
country, the authorities begin to suspect
him. Joe is sent to his aid, and with Joe
given the pianist's pre-recorded brain
patterns, the two swap places during a
radio recital. The pianist is smuggled

out of the country, and Joe is able to
escape the security men who know that
he is not the world class pianist under
suspicion.

## 5. OPERATION McCLAINE

*Screenplay by Gerry Anderson and*
*David Lane*
*Directed by Ken Turner*

A world famous writer is to undergo a
major brain operation, but the brain
surgeon is seriously injured in an
accident, just before he is to perform the
operation. His brain patterns are
transferred to Joe, who successfully
operates in front of unbelieving hospital
staff. But how can his secret be kept?
It's easy, as Mac points out to the staff.
They must take the credit for the
difficult operation. After all, he
explains, who would believe them if
they attributed the success to a nine-
year-old boy?!?

## 8. THE UNORTHODOX SHEPHERD

*Screenplay by Tony Barwick*
*Directed by Ken Turner*

Joe is given the brain patterns of a World Bank President in order to unravel a counterfeit note scandal. It is discovered that a Reverend has been passing the notes. When he is confronted by Joe and Professor McClaine, the Reverend reveals that his verger is being held hostage by the counterfeiters in a church crypt. Joe takes on the role of a ghost and scares the gang of counterfeiters into the arms of waiting police.

## 9. KING FOR A DAY

*Screenplay by Shane Rimmer*
*Directed by Leo Eaton*

When the Sultan of Ardaji is killed, the Regent tries to take over the country by kidnapping the rightful heir to the throne just prior to his coronation. But Joe convincingly takes his place and confuses the situation for long enough for the real heir to be rescued and returned in time to be crowned.

## 10. BUSINESS HOLIDAY

*Screenplay by Tony Barwick*
*Directed by Alan Perry*

After the World Army have evacuated their base in Borova, the local government goes back on its word to leave it empty and begins to use the base for its own ends. Joe takes on the brain patterns of the injured Colonel Henderson, and thus becomes the one person capable of the hazardous military operation necessary to destroy the threatening base.

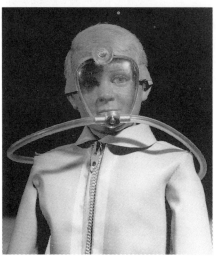

## 6. THE BIG FISH

*Screenplay by Tony Barwick*
*Directed by Alan Perry*

An advanced two-man submarine is laying damaged in forbidden territory and must be recovered without discovery. With the brain patterns of the world's leading aquanaut, Joe dives underwater from a hired boat to move the sub. But when he becomes trapped and does not return to the surface, suspicion falls on Mac and a boat man who are arrested for Joe's murder. Joe first frees himself and moves the sub to safe water, then walks into the jail to prove there is no case against his father and the innocent boatman.

## 7. RELATIVE DANGER

*Screenplay by Shane Rimmer*
*Directed by Peter Anderson*

When Sam Loover's father is trapped underground with two other men, a faster-than-ordinary rescue operation is required - Loover's father suffers from a medical condition that demands regular injections, and without one he will soon die. Sam Loover appeals to Professor McClaine, and Joe is given the brain patterns of a leading underground explorer. After a treacherous journey downward, Joe gets through and administers the vital injection just in time, and soon all are rescued alive.

## 11. MOST SPECIAL ASTRONAUT
*Screenplay by Tony Barwick*
*Directed by Peter Anderson*

With brain patterns transferred from an injured astronaut, Joe is able to save two men in an orbiting space station who are dangerously short of oxygen. But Joe's own journey home becomes perilously dangerous when his spacecraft is damaged, and it requires all of his skills to make it back to Earth safely.

## 12. THREE'S A CROWD
*Screenplay by Tony Barwick*
*Directed by Peter Anderson*

When an extremely lovely reporter by the name of Angela Davis begins to attract Professor McClaine's attention, Sam Loover and Joe become suspicious.

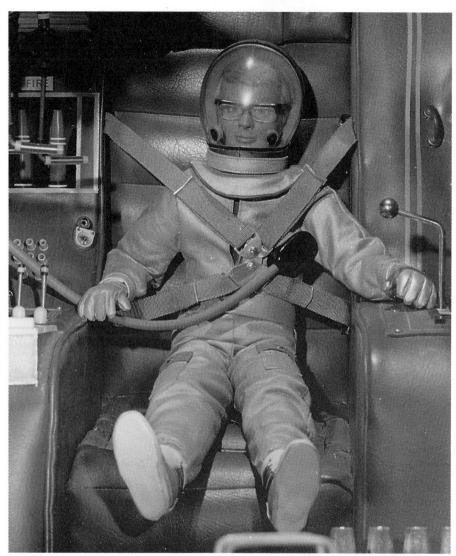

Their fears are confirmed when they discover that she is a foreign agent, and it is finally Joe who sees a way to outwit the scheming Angela without Mac's interference.

## 13. DOUBLE AGENT
*Screenplay by Tony Barwick*
*Directed by Ken Turner*

There have been a number of security breaches in WIN's Courier Department. For a particularly important assignment, Joe is given the brain patterns of Harry Sloane, head of the Department, to ensure complete security. But it turns out that Sloane himself is the traitor who has been causing the security problem, and when he wrests the important package from Joe, the remote control

'destruct' mechanism must be used, and Sloane and the package are destroyed.

## 14. ARCTIC ADVENTURE
*Screenplay by Tony Barwick*
*Directed by Alan Perry*

A World Air Force bomber goes off course in an Arctic storm and is forced to ditch its secret nuclear bombs. But one bomb lands in Eastern Alliance territory and must be recovered to avoid a political incident. With the brain patterns of an elderly sea-bed expert, Joe, in a tiny submarine, is able to search for and locate the bomb, and get it to safety.

## 15. THE FORTRESS
*Screenplay by Shane Rimmer*
*Directed by Leo Eaton*

In the Far Eastern jungle, Joe must be given the brain patterns of a man with vast knowledge of the terrain in order to save the life of one WIN agent, and to prevent the disclosure of the identities of all the others in the area.

## 16. PROJECT 90

*Screenplay by Tony Barwick*
*Directed by Peter Anderson*

Professor McClaine is kidnapped by an international espionage gang who wish to discover the secrets of File 90. They plan to torture him in order to discover those secrets, but Joe comes to his father's rescue. The kidnappers believe they can still get away scot free - until they are suddenly apprehended by Sam Loover and Shane Weston.

## 17. COLONEL McCLAINE

*Screenplay by Tony Barwick*
*Directed by Ken Turner*

Given the brain patterns of an explosives expert and a top army driver, Joe must foil a saboteur's plans during a hazardous trip across Africa - and at the same time prove himself to a private who is astonished by nine-year-old Joe's rank of Colonel!

## 18. LONE-HANDED 90

*Screenplay by Des Saunders*
*and Keith Wilson*
*Directed by Ken Turner*

After falling asleep watching a Western movie on TV, Joe's dreams make him a fast-shooting, tough sheriff, who triumphs in a melodramatic chase against an evil gang, saving the life of his father, Mac!

## 19. THE RACE

*Screenplay by Tony Barwick*
*Directed by Alan Perry*

General Tempest of the World Army issues a challenge to Shane Weston that his organisation can operate more efficiently than WIN. In a land, air and sea race, Joe (with the help of a Monte Carlo rally driver's brain patterns) manages to pass the chequered flag at the finish line for WIN before his opponent from the World Army.

## 20. THE PROFESSIONAL

*Script by Donald James*
*Directed by Leo Eaton*

A revolution in a small country puts a charity's contribution of 10 million dollars worth of gold into the hands of an evil dictator, who will use it to make weapons. Joe uses the brain patterns of a (jailed) professional safecracker to recover the stolen gold!

## 21. TALKDOWN

*Screenplay by Tony Barwick*
*Directed by Alan Perry*

After a test plane has crashed inexplicably and its pilot injured, Joe 90 is given his brain patterns. When Joe makes a test flight in a similar aircraft, the reason for the first crash becomes clear - the pilot had developed a mental block and could not remember the landing procedure! Now all that remains is for Joe to be given the necessary landing instructions from the ground.

## 22. BREAKOUT

*Screenplay by Shane Rimmer*
*Directed by Leo Eaton*

Two convicts escape from a work party in the Canadian mountains, capture the Prime Minister who is visiting nearby, and hold him hostage for a million dollar ransom. But luckily, Joe 90 is on holiday there, and with the brain patterns of an Olympic bobsleigh champion to help him, he is able to rescue the Prime Minister and save the day.

## 23. CHILD OF THE SUN-GOD

*Screenplay by John Lucarotti*
*Directed by Peter Anderson*

When four world statesmen are paralysed by poisoned darts from a blowpipe, Joe is sent to the jungle to

find the Amaztec tribe responsible and bring back an antidote. But it is not so easy. First Joe has to outwit the white man who has been posing as the Amaztec god, and beat him at his own game....

## 24. TRIAL AT SEA

*Screenplay by Donald James*
*Directed by Leo Eaton*

A disgruntled ex-employee threatens the maiden voyage of the new 'Hoverliner'. But the saboteur (who has planted explosives somewhere aboard the ship) is apprehended and his brain patterns recorded. Now it's time for the bomb to be located and disarmed - and with the brain patterns transferred to him, Joe is just the boy for the job.

## 25. VIVA CORDOVA

*Screenplay by Tony Barwick*
*Directed by Peter Anderson*

Cordova, a man just elected President of his country, refuses to have bodyguards. But his life is threatened and he must be protected. With the right brain patterns

bomb in orbit and hold the world to ransom, WIN must take action. Joe pilots the Air Force's most heavily - armed fighter bomber to the rocket launch site, and after several attempts, in a desperate final dive, he hits the already-fuelled rocket and destroys the complex.

### 27. MISSION X-14

*Screenplay by*
*Gerry and Sylvia Anderson*
*Written by Pat Dunlop*
*Directed by Ken Turner*

It is vital that WIN obtains the antibody that can stop the new virus X-14, which

is capable of breaking down the molecular structure of a building. Joe is dispatched to an enemy research station where he discovers the formula for the antibody, and audaciously returns home in an enemy aircraft that he has stolen.

### 28. TEST FLIGHT

*Screenplay by*
*Gerry and Sylvia Anderson*
*Written by Donald James*
*Directed by Peter Anderson*

After a series of sabotage attempts on the new Orbital Glide Transport aircraft, the saboteur is identified. But the man escapes and tries to destroy the only

proof that incriminates him. It takes all of Joe's skill (and the brain patterns of a computer and explosives expert) to bring the fugitive to justice.

### 29. SEE YOU DOWN THERE

*Screenplay by*
*Gerry and Sylvia Anderson*
*Written by Tony Barwick*
*Directed by Leo Eaton*

By using the remarkable power that allows him to take on several different brain patterns one after another, and use skills that no nine-year-old could ever ordinarily have, Joe is able to effect a

shock conversion of a financial shark into a man who swears that he will be honest in future.

### 30. THE BIRTHDAY

*Screenplay by*
*Gerry and Sylvia Anderson*
*Written by Tony Barwick*
*Directed by Leo Eaton*

It's Joe's birthday - he is ten years old! Over tea and a huge birthday cake, Joe discusses with Mac, Sam and Shane his missions for WIN and remembers them in exciting flashbacks. At the end of the day the toast is to Joe 90 - WIN's Most Special Agent!

in his nine-year-old body, Joe is able to do the job without the President suspecting. Nor is the President aware that Joe thwarts four attempts on his life and ends the threat of assassination!

### 26. ATTACK OF THE TIGER

*Screenplay by*
*Gerry and Sylvia Anderson*
*Written by Tony Barwick*
*Directed by Peter Anderson*

When an enemy power is discovered in the throes of a plan to put a nuclear

Principal Credits
30 thirty minute episodes
Colour
A Century 21 Production in association
with ATV for ITC World-Wide
Distribution
Created by Gerry and Sylvia Anderson
Executive Producer : Reg Hill
Producer : David Lane
Script Editor : Tony Barwick
Supervising Visual Effects Director:
Derek Meddings
Music composer and director:
 Barry Gray
Puppet Co-ordinator: Mary Turner

1969

# SECRET SERVICE

## Characters

FATHER STANLEY UNWIN - the country vicar who is also a secret agent
MATTHEW HARDING - posing as Unwin's gardener, he is in fact a top agent himself, ready to be miniaturised whenever a case demands it
THE BISHOP - the codename of a senior member of British Intelligence in Whitehall
MRS APPLEBY - Father Unwin's house-keeper

## Voices

Father Unwin ...... Stanley Unwin
Matthew ...... Gary Files
The Bishop ...... Jeremy Wilkin
Mrs Appleby ...... Sylvia Anderson

## Premise

When a late member of his parish leaves Father Stanley Unwin a strange briefcase, it unexpectedly changes Unwin's life. Inside the briefcase is a miniaturisation device, and the parishioner's request is that Father Unwin uses it as he sees fit for the good of mankind. Father Unwin decides to use this 'Minimiser' - which can shrink objects or people to one-third of their normal size - to aid British Intelligence. Father Unwin's contact there is the BISHOP - British Intelligence Service Headquarters Operation Priest. Operating out of his home, the Vicarage, and driving his 1917 Model 'T' Ford, and with the assistance of a reducible agent, Father Unwin becomes a vital contributor to British security!

# 1. A CASE FOR THE BISHOP

*Teleplay by Gerry and Sylvia Anderson*
*Directed by Alan Perry*

It's a case for the Bishop when a foreign ambassador plans to leave the country with a stolen computer prototype. The Bishop contacts Father Unwin, who minimises Matthew and stows him away in the Ambassador's aircraft. After the plane takes off, Matthew switches off the engines. The plane is forced to land in a deserted airfield, where the Ambassador is confronted by Father Unwin, who soon recovers both the stolen computer prototype and Matthew.

# 2. A QUESTION OF MIRACLES

*Teleplay by Donald James*
*Directed by Leo Eaton*

A series of accidents at British-made desalinisation plants is threatening export orders for the plant and causing anxiety to all involved, so Father Unwin is brought in. He and Matthew proceed to the next-most-likely scene of attack. They successfully deceive everyone, most importantly the villains, and are thus able to discover a bomb in some vital machinery, a sabotage plot, and the mastermind behind it all.

# 3. TO CATCH A SPY

*Teleplay by Tony Barwick*
*Directed by Brian Heard*

A man sentenced to a long term of imprisonment for spying escapes and hides out with the sympathetic Sir Humphrey Burton, a man of considerable influence. But the fugitive is a threat and must be apprehended - otherwise he could cause the total collapse of the British defence system!

It takes Father Unwin's sensitive approach to get into Sir Humphrey's house, and there the minimised Matthew uncovers a plot to smuggle the spy out of the country by submarine. Armed with this information Father Unwin arranges for the submarine to be scared off and survives a dangerous confrontation with a gun-wielding Sir Humphrey.

# 4. THE FEATHERED SPIES

*Teleplay by Tony Barwick*
*Directed by Peter Anderson*

It seems impossible that aerial photographs of a secret British installation have been offered for sale on the international espionage market when no aircraft have been seen to fly over it. But with Father Unwin's keen investigation the answer becomes clear - a miniature camera attached to a homing pigeon has been doing the job. At the home of the pigeon's owner, a miniaturised Matthew has to overcome a large dog. Now time is running short - another pigeon carrying a bomb is heading towards the installation, and must be stopped!

# 5. LAST TRAIN TO BUFFLERS HALT

*Teleplay by Tony Barwick*
*Directed by Alan Perry*

After an attempt by highwaymen to steal a consignment of gold travelling by British Rail, Father Unwin is engaged to accompany the train. The bandits, led by a traitorous British Rail official, try again, and this time succeed, by diverting the train to a disused station at Bufflers Halt. But while they are waiting for trucks to arrive to carry the gold away, Father Unwin and the miniaturised Matthew outwit the crooks and lock them in a security van.

# 6. HOLE IN ONE

*Teleplay by Shane Rimmer*
*Directed by Brian Heard*

A sabotage team who seem to have access to inside information are methodically preventing every attempt

to correct the orbit of an important satellite. With the minaturised Matthew's help, Father Unwin discovers that a General has unknowingly been giving away the information the saboteurs need on the golf course - his golf balls have been bugged! A final attempt is to be made to correct the satellite's orbit, and the saboteurs must be rendered inoperative. Father Unwin arranges another golf game with the General, and plans to substitute a golf ball with a gas capsule in it to put to sleep the saboteurs in their underground hide-out. But time is running out and the ball must go into the 15th hole - it must be a hole in one!

# 7. RECALL TO SERVICE

*Teleplay by Pat Dunlop*
*Directed by Peter Anderson*

Father Unwin is invited to try and prevent a possible sabotage at a demonstration of the Army's latest and most advanced tank and he goes disguised as an Army padre. As the exercise progresses, it becomes clear to

Father Unwin that someone has programmed the tank to attack the blockhouse where top NATO officials are watching. He goes to the control room where he finds that a senior officer has destroyed the computer and the tank can no longer be remote controlled nor stopped from its destructive mission. Now he must give instructions to Matthew (who he has stowed away in the tank) as to how to stop the machine manually - a difficult task manipulating the heavy controls for the miniaturised gardener!

## 8. ERRAND OF MERCY

*Teleplay by Tony Barwick*
*Directed by Leo Eaton*

Confined to bed with an illness, Father Unwin is plied with medicine by his housekeeper, Mrs Appleby. But the medicine proves to be somewhat of a stimulant, and Father Unwin begins to hallucinate... he imagines that he and Matthew undertake a mission to get vital medical supplies to a plague area.... as they complete the mission, Father Unwin wakes up.....it's morning and the whole adventure nothing more than a dream.

## 9. THE DEADLY WHISPER

*Teleplay by Donald James*
*Directed by Leo Eaton*

Father Unwin becomes suspicious when a friend who has previously been a prize-winning rose-grower suddenly changes to dahlias. He soon discovers that the man is being held captive, and that a sonic rifle he has invented is to be used against a new jet fighter. Father Unwin causes the plan to rebound on the captors by arranging for a hypersonic aircraft to fly over the area, creating a sonic boom which destroys the rifle.

## 10. THE CURE

*Teleplay by Pat Dunlop*
*Directed by Leo Eaton*

The notorious international agent Sakov has surprisingly turned up at a Health Centre close to a site where a new fuel is to be tested in a racing car under the eye of a Government Minister. Father Unwin checks in for a cure at the Health Centre, where he begins a rather strenuous course of treatment. This involves his being strapped down and completely immobilized - and it is while he is in this helpless position that Sakov confides to him that he has already sabotaged the car, and it will explode as soon as the new fuel is used. Father Unwin must escape from the Health Centre and get Matthew to stop the car test - somehow - before it's too late!

## 11. SCHOOL FOR SPIES

*Teleplay by Donald James*
*Directed by Ken Turner*

A gang posing as priests have been responsible for a great deal of sabotage. Father Unwin decides to infiltrate the gang, and after succeeding at some difficult tests he is accepted as a member. But his identity is uncovered and he is put on the wrong end of the gang's next sabotage mission - tied up in a motor launch full of explosives which is on a collision course with a nuclear submarine. But Matthew sneaks on board to save him, and with the aid of the police, the gang are captured.

## 12. MAY-DAY, MAY-DAY!

Teleplay by Bob Keston
Directed by Alan Perry

An Arab king is in London to sign an important oil concession. But certain factions in his country oppose the deal, and his life is under threat. One attempt is made (and foiled by Matthew) while the king sleeps. But when the king leaves by plane for New York, the trouble really starts. Father Unwin and Matthew have to find and dispose of a bomb that has been placed aboard, and then Father Unwin must take the controls - the crew have been gassed - and land the plane in Iceland. Father Unwin, who has never flown before, has to be talked down by Air Traffic Controllers, which leads to several near-disasters.

## 13. MORE HASTE - LESS SPEED

*Teleplay by Tony Barwick*
*Directed by Ken Turner*

When Mullins, a counterfeiter, is released from prison, the Bishop sends Father Unwin after him in the hope that the vital printing plates, that were never recovered, can now be found. But when Mullins returns to his gang, who hold one of the two plates, they torture him and make him reveal where the missing plate is. Soon all four members of the gang know where the plate is (hidden in a barn), and are competing to get to it first. But after they have listened in to the proceedings, Father Unwin and Matthew use the advantages of miniaturisation to get the plates while the gang fight amongst themselves.

### Principal Credits

13 thirty minute episodes
Colour
A Century 21 Production in association with ATV for ITC World-Wide Distribution
Series Created by Gerry and Sylvia Anderson
Executive Producer: Reg Hill
Producer: David Lane
Visual Effects Supervisor: Derek Meddings
Script Editor: Tony Barwick
Music Composer and Conductor: Barry Gray
Puppetry Co-ordinator: Mary Turner

1970

Unidentified Flying Objects - a menace from outer space! It is the 1980s, and UFOs are a reality. They are believed to be a threat to Earth, and a highly organised defence system has been set up. Completely secret, with a base on the moon and concealed underground headquarters in England, it is named SHADO - Supreme Headquarters, Alien Defence Organisation.
It is the duty of the SHADO personnel, led by Ed Straker, to protect the Earth from the deadly UFO invaders.

## Major characters

COMMANDER ED STRAKER -
SHADO's dedicated leader
COLONEL ALEC FREEMAN -
Straker's number two
PAUL FOSTER - the pilot who
discovered SHADO's work and was
then recruited by them
CAPTAIN PETER CARLIN - pilot of
the interceptor Skydiver 1
LT GAY ELLIS - Commander of
Moonbase Control
GENERAL HENDERSON - the man
who founded SHADO

## Cast

Commander Straker .... Ed Bishop
Colonel Freeman .... George Sewell
Paul Foster .... Michael Billington
Captain Carlin .... Peter Gordeno
Miss Ealand .... Norma Ronald
Lt Mark Bradley .... Harry Baird
Lt Lew Waterman .... Gary Myers
Lt Joan Harrington.... Antonia Ellis
Lt Nina Barry .... Dolores Mantez
Lt Ford .... Keith Alexander
Lt Gay Ellis .... Gabrielle Drake
Col Virginia Lake .... Wanda Ventham
Gen Henderson .... Grant Taylor
Dr Jackson .... Vladek Sheybal
Miss Holland .... Lois Maxwell

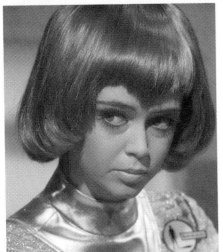

## 1. IDENTIFIED
*Teleplay by Gerry and Sylvia Anderson with Tony Barwick*
*Directed by Gerry Anderson*

Peter Carlin's sister has disappeared after contact with an alien craft. So he is especially pleased when, as a member of SHADO, he uses new equipment to intercept a UFO for the first time. The UFO crashes, and its pilot's body is rushed to hospital - but too late to save him. As soon as the alien's helmet is removed, the face's youthful features are transformed into those of an incredibly aged man, and he dies. But the alien's body holds a terrible secret - many of its

organs are human! The aliens, a dying race, are in desperate need of replacement organs from healthy people. They have been finding their hopes of survival on Earth, millions of miles away, by raids in search of human organs to keep themselves alive. Commander Straker has to break the horrifying news to Captain Carlin - the dead alien has the transplanted heart of his sister.

## 2. EXPOSED
*Teleplay by Tony Barwick*
*Directed by Dave Lane*

When a civilian test pilot named Paul Foster sees and photographs a UFO, it is felt it may be a danger to SHADO. A major part of their job is to prevent the mass hysteria and terror that could be caused by confirmation of the existence of UFOs. So a major operation is undertaken to nullify the threat represented by Paul Foster - until he is finally convinced to join SHADO himself.

## 3. SURVIVAL
*Teleplay by Tony Barwick*
*Directed by Alan Perry*

When a UFO lands somewhere on the moon a search is ordered to find it. But it means disaster for Paul Foster when the UFO is spotted, and shot down - it crashes on his moonmobile and he is left for dead. But though his transport is destroyed, Paul is alive.... and so is the alien! Using Paul's gun, the alien forces Paul to lead the way to the Moonbase - until his air supply runs out. Then, incredibly, the alien gives Paul one of his own oxygen canisters to continue the journey. But tragedy lies ahead.....

## 4. CONFLICT
*Teleplay by Ruric Powell*
*Directed by Ken Turner*

Ed Straker is convinced that space debris - discarded rocket boosters and other junk - is both a danger and a cover for alien activity. But even after the deaths of two SHADO spacemen, he is unable to convince General Henderson of the International Astrophysical Commission to resolve the problem. By the time Straker takes Henderson to SHADO HQ to prove his point, it may be too late - they will only be able to clear away the debris if they can survive the attack of the UFO that is homing in on them from behind it!

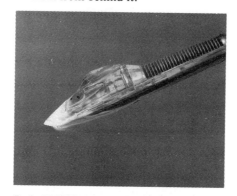

## 5. A QUESTION OF PRIORITIES
*Teleplay by Tony Barwick*
*Directed by David Lane*

A terrible choice is facing Ed Straker. His son lies critically injured after a road accident and is in need of drugs that will

have to be transported from America. In Ireland, an alien wants to defect to Earth, and needs to be saved from a UFO that is chasing him, but there is only one SHADO air transporter available for both tasks. Which should he choose? To save his dying son, or rescue the defecting alien who may have vital information that would protect the world?

## 6. THE SQUARE TRIANGLE
*Teleplay by Alan Pattillo*
*Directed by David Lane*
*Guest Stars:*
*Adrienne Corri  as Liz Newton*
*Patrick Mower as Cass Fowler*

Liz Newton and her lover, Cass Fowler, are waiting in a forest cottage for the arrival of Liz's husband, Jack, so that she can shoot him, and then claim that she thought it was an intruder. So when an alien (who Straker has allowed to land in England) arrives, they are extremely surprised. When Paul Foster and a SHADO search party turn up, hot on the alien's heels, the two lovers are taken into custody. It's quite a quandary for Ed Straker and Colonel Freeman now; the couple have seen an alien and must therefore have all recollections of him erased with an amnesia drug. This means that they will remember nothing of the past 24 hours and will be back where they were - planning Jack Newton's murder....!

## 7. ORDEAL

*Teleplay by Tony Barwick*
*Directed by Ken Turner*

The day after an indulgent night out at a party, Paul Foster goes for a check-up at the SHADO Health Farm. When he gets into the sauna his hangover really begins to take effect. He passes into a semi-conscious state and becomes aware of strange events around him. He is kidnapped by a UFO, given an alien helmet, and left on the moon. SHADO finds him - but how can they remove the helmet without losing the breathing liquid that is now giving him life? Paul finds himself fighting to live - until he realises he is just becoming conscious again, still in the sauna bath!

## 8. E.S.P.

*Teleplay by Alan Fennell*
*Director by Ken Turner*
*With Guest Stars:*
*John Stratton as Croxley*
*Deborah Stanford as Stella Croxley*

John Croxley has E.S.P. - extra sensory perception - and his powers are so pronounced that he can <u>feel</u> the future. When his wife Stella is killed by a UFO crash, he is determined to get revenge. He lures Straker and Freeman to his house, intent on killing them. They are defenceless - because he can anticipate their every thought and movement. Soon the truth (and Croxley's unpleasant

motivation) becomes clear; his mind has been taken over by the aliens from outer space. Only Paul Foster can save the other two SHADO men now!

## 9. CLOSE UP

*Teleplay by Tony Barwick*
*Directed by Alan Perry*

An operation is launched to photograph the aliens' home planet by having an extremely powerful and accurate telescope track a UFO as it leaves Earth and goes home. But a SHADO scientist with a different project involving micro-photography has been refused funding that has been used for the telescope. By a cunning manoeuvre, he gets a chance to show some new data to Straker who is enthralled. With the promise that his project would produce more of this fascinating information, the scientist at last gets a guarantee of money for his project.

## 10. COURT MARTIAL

*Teleplay by Tony Barwick*
*Directed by Ron Appleton*

All the evidence points to Paul Foster being the man who has been giving away SHAD0 secrets. He is court-martialled and sentenced to death. But Straker is unable to believe Foster's guilt and investigates further. At Foster's home he discovers a bugging device, and when he finds that the bug was planted by an industrial spy trying to learn secrets of Paul's 'cover' career as movie executive, the innocent Paul is freed.

## 11. CONFETTI CHECK A-O.K.

*Teleplay by Tony Barwick*
*Directed by David Lane*
*With Suzanne Neve as Mary Straker*

When a SHADO operative's wife gives birth to twins, it triggers in Straker bitter memories of his own marriage to Mary. Just after their honeymoon began, the first UFO attack was made on General Henderson, and Straker was ordered to set up and command SHADO. But it was a secret mission he dare not tell his new wife about. As months passed, Straker spent less and less time at home, and just before the birth of their baby, the final straw came for Mary. She learns that Ed Straker has been seen leaving a girl's flat late at night - and Ed can't explain because the girl was in fact a SHADO operative and they were having a vitally important meeting. It is the end of Straker's marriage.... Mary cares only for the baby.

## 12. KILL STRAKER

*Teleplay by Donald James*
*Directed by Alan Perry*

Following a UFO attack on Paul Foster and Frank Craig in a lunar module, these two previously loyal men begin to wage a campaign of words against Straker, alleging that he is incompetent and obsessed with his command. Things become more serious when Craig attempts to murder Straker, but he fails. Foster then provokes a showdown with Straker - a battle that Straker wins.

During psychiatric treatment, Foster reveals the strange truth - the UFO attack had subjected the two men to a deep subliminal impulse which made them intent on destroying Straker, which would weaken SHADO and leave Earth vulnerable to an imminent outer space attack.

## 13. SUB-SMASH

*Teleplay by Alan Fennell*
*Directed by David Lane*
*With Dolores Mantez as Lt Nina Barry*

While investigating a new form of UFO that can attack underwater, a team of SHADO operatives are endangered when their craft, the new Skydiver, is bombed by the undersea UFO. Most members of the crew are evacuated, but

the escape hatch jams and Straker and Lt Nina Barry are trapped. She is badly injured and both are close to death. In what they think must be their last moments, the two become very close to each other, breaking through the barrier of reserve that had separated them through the years they have worked together in SHADO. But salvation comes, and the two are rescued. Afterwards, as they recover, Nina can't help wondering if, in her moment of vulnerability, she said too much...

## 14. THE DALOTEK AFFAIR

*Teleplay by Ruric Powell*
*Directed by Alan Perry*
*With Tracy Reed as Jane Carson*

When the visit of a team of three lunar surveyors from a private business corporation, headed by Jane Carson,

coincides with an inexplicable temporary failure of radio and video equipment around Moonbase, Straker is extremely suspicious. Second and third failures (each time cutting the video link with Earth and the alien detection system) do nothing to alleviate his suspicions. But after the third attack, Jane Carson and her colleagues themselves discover the cause of the problem - some very strange equipment in a deep crater caused by a recent meteorite crash.

## 15. FLIGHT PATH

*Teleplay by Ian Scott*
*Directed by Ken Turner*
*Guest Artists:*
*George Cole as Roper*
*Sonia Fox as Carol*

With his wife Carol threatened by a mystery man, SHADO's Paul Roper begins to pass on secret information that would aid a major UFO attack. But when he begins to supply false information, his wife is attacked. Roper decides to try and redeem himself, but he has already given away too much information. The UFOs are going to attack at the same time as some sunspot activity. The attackers will be undetectable - except to one man, stationed at a certain position on the Moon's surface. It is Roper's chance to get his revenge by frustrating the attackers he has aided, and saving the friends he has betrayed.

## 16. THE COMPUTER AFFAIR

*Teleplay by Tony Barwick*
*Directed by David Lane*
*With Harry Baird as Lt Bradley*
*Gabrielle Drake as Lt Ellis*

In a tragic defeat for SHADO, a UFO manages to get past three interceptors, destroying one, and through Earth's outer defences. Straker orders Gay Ellis, who issued the unsuccessful evasive instructions, and the two remaining pilots to be psychoanalysed and the results fed into a computer. The computer's astonishing verdict - that Gay Ellis and one of the pilots, Mark Bradley, are in love, and Gay's misjudgement was caused by worry over Mark's safety. When the two are posted together again, this time in search of trespassing UFO, they must avoid a repeat of the previous incident.

## 17. THE RESPONSIBILITY SEAT

*Teleplay by Tony Barwick*
*Directed by Alan Perry*
*Guest Artist:*
*Jane Merrow as Jo Fraser*

Jo Fraser, a reporter, interviews Straker in his cover role as a film producer. But when he discovers that she is not from the newspaper she claimed to represent, he decides to go after her. Meanwhile, he leaves Colonel Freeman in charge of SHADO. Both of them learn quite a lesson - for Straker, the attractive reporter turns out to be a dangerous risk; and Freeman learns that the responsibility seat is a hot one to sit in!

her giving away too much information, or it may be too late to prevent UFOs from finding the containers and releasing the gas - thereby destroying every form of life on Earth!

## 18. THE CAT WITH TEN LIVES

*Teleplay by David Tomblin*
*Directed by David Tomblin*
*Special Guest Artist:*
*Alexis Kanner as Regan*
*With Geraldine Moffat as Jean Regan*

When SHADO interceptor pilot Regan and his wife Jean find a Siamese cat in the road, it spells trouble for them. First Jean is abducted by UFOs. Then Regan begins to go crazy, in a frenzy which reaches a climax when he knocks Col Foster unconscious. It's Straker who first realises that Regan is being turned into an automaton by the cat, which is in fact an alien being that has Regan in its power. The first step of the solution will be to catch the escaped cat - by sending a pack of dogs after it!

## 19. THE SOUND OF SILENCE

*Teleplay by David Lane and Bob Bell*
*Directed by David Lane*
*Guest Star: Michael Jayston as Russ*

Some sinister and mysterious questions come to light following a series of strange UFO experiences. International showjumping champion Russ Stone disappears; the horribly mutilated bodies of a local drop-out and his dogs are found, and the UFOs are seen present. When SHADO depth-charges a UFO that has fallen into a lake, a cigar-shaped cylinder is the only thing that comes to surface. What, or <u>who</u> does it contain?

## 20. DESTRUCTION

*Teleplay by Dennis Spooner*
*Directed by Ken Turner*
*Guest Stars:*
*Stephanie Beacham as Sarah Bosanquet*
*Edwin Richfield as*
*Admiral Sheringham*

Under the command of Admiral Sheringham, the Navy has been dumping into the sea containers of an experimental nerve gas which proved to be far too dangerous to be even used. But SHADO discovers that the Admiral's secretary, Sarah Bosanquet, has been subverted by the aliens through a powerful telescope with which she watches the skies. Either they must stop

## 21. THE MAN WHO CAME BACK

*Teleplay by Terence Feely*
*Directed by David Lane*
*Guest stars:*
*Derren Nesbitt as Craig Collins*
*Gary Raymond as Col Grey*

Spaceship pilot Craig Collins disappears while making re-entry into the atmosphere and is believed dead. However after two months, he suddenly turns up in the South Pacific. He is immediately put back to work on SHADO's SID satellite computer, on which he is an expert. But after attacking Virginia Lake, Paul Foster and Colonel Grey, it becomes clear that something is very wrong with Collins. Tests show that his personality centres have been destroyed by laser beam surgery and that he has been programmed by the aliens who did it so that he can be controlled with sound waves. All that remains is to alert Straker in time - he is on a mission with Collins, who has been programmed to kill him!

## 22. THE PSYCHOBOMBS

*Teleplay by Tony Barwick*
*Directed by Jeremy Summers*
*Guest stars:*
*Deborah Grant as Linda*
*Mike Pratt as Mason*
*David Collings as Clark*

Three ordinary people are taken over by UFOs and given superhuman powers with which they are to destroy SHADO. Clark, a bank clerk, uses his superhuman strength to break in and destroy the Fairfield Tracker Station. Then Mason, a motorway construction manager, gets aboard Skydiver Three and blows it to smithereens. Now Linda, a secretary already responsible for two murders, must be stopped before she can destroy Commander Straker and SHADO Control.

## 23. MINDBENDER

*Teleplay by Tony Barwick*
*Directed by Ken Turner*

A UFO comes within three miles of
Moonbase, and then blows itself up.
And all that can be found at the scene is
a diamond-like rock. But when one of
the SHADO men brings the rock back
into Moonbase, the trouble begins -
because anyone who touches the deadly
moon rock believes that everyone they
see - even their closest friends - are
aliens to be destroyed.

## 24. REFLECTIONS IN THE WATER

*Teleplay by David Tomblin*
*Directed by David Tomblin*

Investigating reports of explosive
imitation flying fish in the Atlantic,
Straker and Foster find a huge dome
underwater. Inside the dome they find
an exact replica of SHADO
headquarters, including exact replica
people. When they hear the imitation
HQ giving instructions to Moonbase to
permit a huge invasion by UFOs, they
realise that the fake HQ in the dome has
been successfully deceiving Moonbase,
and something must be done....fast!

## 25. THE LONG SLEEP

*Teleplay by David Tomblin*
*Directed by Jeremy Summers*
*Guest Artists:*
*Tessa Wyatt as Catherine*
*Christian Roberts as Tim*

A girl named Catherine begins to
recover from a ten-year-long coma,
originally caused by a road accident in
which Straker was involved. She begins
to recall events just prior to her accident,
and tells them to the men from
SHADO. A man named Tim... an
encounter with aliens... a bomb buried at
a farmhouse... suddenly the ten-year-old
mystery attains a new urgency when it is
discovered that the man Tim is alive and
under alien control. He is planning to
find the farm and explode the deadly
bomb - and he must be stopped!

## 26. TIMELASH

*Teleplay by Terence Feely*
*Directed by Cyril Frankel*
*Guest Artist: Patrick Allen as Turner*

As Straker returns to SHADO
headquarters with Virginia Lake, they
notice that everything around them is
totally still, frozen in time. They only
prevent the same thing happening to
themselves when Straker rushes to the
laboratory and injects them with a
chemical solution to speed up their
actions. Suddenly, a challenge rings out.
The time stoppage is the latest attempt
by aliens to destroy Straker and
SHADO, engineered by the human,
Turner. Now Straker, Virginia, and the
evil Turner must battle it out in a
timeless moment in which no-one else
can interfere!

### Principal Credits

26 sixty minute episodes
Colour
A Century 21 Pictures Production for
ITC World Wide Distribution
Produced by Reg Hill
Executive Producer : Gerry Anderson
Format by Gerry and Sylvia Anderson
with Reg Hill
Art Director : Bob Bell

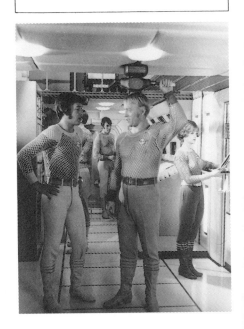

1972

The Protectors are a world-wide freelance detective/crime-fighting organisation, who hire their services out to any governments, businesses or wealthy individuals who can afford them.

Three of their European operatives are Harry Rule, Contessa Caroline Di Contini and Paul Buchet. They are constantly involved in kidnappings, industrial wrangles, diplomatic problems, and no end of other challenges - ensuring adventure and excitement for the trio!

## Characters

HARRY RULE - the cool, professional Protector, based in London
CONTESSA CAROLINE DI CONTINI - an expert in art and antique thefts; lives in a villa in Rome
PAUL BUCHET - youngest of the three, lives in 'swinging' Paris
SUKI (1st season only) - Harry's au pair girl, and a judo expert
CHINO (1st season only) - the Contessa's oriental driver, a karate expert

## Cast

Harry Rule....Robert Vaughn
Contessa Di Contini...
Nyree Dawn Porter
Paul Buchet....Tony Anholt
Suki....Yasuko Nazagumi
Chino....Anthony Chinn

## 1. 2000 FT. TO DIE

*Screenplay by Terence Feeley*
*Directed by John Hough*

The services of Harry, the Contessa and Paul are engaged to protect the life of the only man who knows the secret of synthetic gold creation. Someone known only as 'Man Three' is out to kill him and the first attack will be when he attempts a dangerous sky-diving stunt.

## 2. BROTHER HOOD

*Screenplay by John Goldsmith*
*Directed by Don Chaffey*
*Guest Artists:*
*Vladek Sheybal as Sandor Karoleon*
*Patrick Troughton as Bela Karoleon*

Bela Karoleon arranges for the Protectors to spring his brother Sandor

from a foreign jail. But when this is done, they discover that Bela's motives are not benignly fraternal - in fact, Sandor is one of the few men who know that Bela's 'Karoleon Corporation' is a front for the biggest illegal drug operation in the world, and Bela wants his brother dead.

## 3. DISAPPEARING TRICK

*Screenplay by Brian Clemens*
*Directed by Jeremy Summers*
*Guest Artists:*
*David Bauer as Carl Huron*
*Derren Nesbitt as Brad Huron*

The Contessa takes her life in her hands when she agrees to try and hide Brad Huron somewhere on Earth where he can't be found. Unknown to the Contessa, Brad is a homicidal maniac, as his father Carl Huron soon reveals to Harry and Paul. Now they have to try and find the Contessa.... but how can they track down such an excellent Protector?

## 4. YOUR WITNESS

*Screenplay by Donald James*
*Directed by Jeremy Summers*
*Guest Artists:*
*George Baker as Dixon*
*Stephanie Beacham as Christie*

Christie, the key witness in a Paris murder case, needs to be protected, according to her guardian Dixon.

However, Christie seems determined to resist the Protectors' attention, and gives them the slip. Soon it's revealed the the murdered man had taken part in a big bullion robbery.... so it's even more important that the evasive Christie be found.

## 5. THE QUICK BROWN FOX

*Screenplay by Donald James*
*Directed by Don Chaffey*
*With Morris Perry as Keller*

It seems that Hans Keller, a convicted Nazi war criminal, is the paymaster for a pension scheme for five other undercover Nazis. The Protectors are sent on a mission by the West German government to find the infamous five, and it seems the key to the matter is in a coded message sent by Keller that must be deciphered. But all it says is 'The quick brown fox jumps over the lazy dog'. What can it mean?

## 6. THE NUMBERS GAME

*Screenplay by Ralph Smart*
*Directed by Don Chaffey*

The wealthy father of a runaway girl has engaged the Protectors to persuade his daughter to return home. When they find her, she is living on money earned by merely passing on lists of numbers by telephone. The numbers form a code, and breaking the code leads Harry and the Contessa into a web of intrigue, at the centre of which they come face-to-face with the head of an international smuggling operation.

## 7. TRIPLE CROSS

*Screenplay by Lew Davidson*
*Directed by John Hough*
*Guest Artist: John Neville as Charlie*

A man called Charlie kidnaps Paul, and in return for his release he wants Harry and the Contessa to steal some jewels. They do it and then go after Charlie, only to find him dead. Now they have to try and find the missing jewellery, the missing Paul, and a bomb that is going to explode in five minutes!

## 8. A KIND OF WILD JUSTICE

*Screenplay by Donald James*
*Directed by Jeremy Summers*
*Guest Artists:*
*Anna Palk as Kate*
*Patrick O'Connell as Reagan.*

Harry unwittingly becomes part of a bizarre plan masterminded by Kate Lindeman, a dead racketeer's daughter. She tricks him into finding her father's gang, now headed by a man called Reagan. At first, she demands £100,000 as compensation for her father's death from the new gang leader. But when she

suddenly pulls a gun on Reagan, it's time for the Protectors to join the fray!

## 9. ONE AND ONE MAKES ONE

*Screenplay by Jesse and Pat Lasky*
*Directed by Don Chaffey*
*Guest Artists:*
*Michael Gough as Shkoder*
*Georgia Brown as Maria Ghardala*

A foreign agent named Kosneff has been assigned to kill Canadian agent Bennett, and then take his place by using plastic surgery to impersonate him. Harry wants to locate the real Bennett, who has some important secret information. But when he does find him, how is he going to discover if this Bennett is the genuine one?

## 10. SEE NO EVIL

*Screenplay by Donald Jonson*
*Directed by Jeremy Summers*
*Guest Artists:*
*James Bolam as Max*
*Alan Webb as The Blind Man*

A senator in Rome is heading a new investigative commission that is planning to suppress organised crime. But the senator is kidnapped, drugged, and some very incriminating photographs of him are taken. It's going to be a hard task for the Protectors to prevent a blackmail attempt and recover the photographic negatives, so that the Senator can continue his crime-busting duties.

## 11. BALANCE OF TERROR

*Screenplay by John Goldsmith*
*Directed by Don Chaffey*
*Guest Artists:*
*Nigel Green as Krassinkov*
*Laurence Naismith as Schelpin*

Defecting Russian scientist Professor Schelpin is in London to warn of the dangers of germ warfare. But he plans to do it by proving the deadly power of such weapons - using a single phial of a toxic chemical to kill the millions who live in England's capital city. The Protectors must stop him, to preserve peace and the international balance of power.

## 12. KING CON

*Screenplay by Tony Barwick*
*Directed by Jeremy Summers*
*Guest Artist:*
*Anton Rodgers as Sutherland*

When a friend is swindled by a confidence trickster named Sutherland, the Contessa is determined to get her own back. First, she buys back her friend's valuable artefact at an exorbitant price. Then, with the help of Harry and a Czechoslovakian Protector, she cons Sutherland himself and gets all the money back!

## 13. THE BIG HIT

*Screenplay by Donald James*
*Directed by Roy Ward Baker*
*Guest Artist:*
*Derek Smith as Jason Howard*

After the deaths of two Protectors in New York and Tokyo, followed by an attempt on the Contessa's life, it is clear that there is a plot afoot to destroy all the members of the Protectors organisation. Then Harry is kidnapped, and it is up to Paul and the Contessa to follow up some slim leads in order to save Harry and end the campaign being masterminded by Jason Howard against the Protectors.

## 14. THINK BACK

*Screenplay by Brain Clemens*
*Directed by Cyril Frankel*
*Guest Artist:*
*Ian Hendry as Inspector Wilson*

In a complex criminal operation Harry and the Contessa are deceived into believing they have been in a car crash. Then they are questioned by Inspector Wilson, in fact a fake policeman, who discovers the location of a man the two are supposed to be protecting. But when Harry and the Contessa realise they have been set up and tricked, they have to race against the false inspector to save the man in their care.

## 15. THE FIRST CIRCLE

*Screenplay by Tony Barwick*
*Directed by Don Chaffey*
*Guest Artists:*
*Ed Bishop as Hunter*
*John Collin as Slade*

Colonel John Hunter, a U.S. Air Force veteran of the Vietnam war, is now living in England. It is his wife who contacts Harry when Hunter begins to re-live, in his mind, the torment of his war experiences. But by the time Harry arrives, it is too late. Hunter has gone crazy and is living in a fantasy world where he must destroy the Vietcong enemy. He finally creates his own downfall by trying to fly - in a jeep!

## 16. CHASE

*Screenplay by Brian Clemens*
*Directed by Harry Booth*
*Guest Artists:*
*Patrick Magee as Garder*
*Keith Buckley as Kurt*

Harry and the Contessa accidentally become victims of a gang of South American terrorists headed by the ruthless Garder. While staying in the forests of Northern Europe, a wounded diplomat strays into the house of the two Protectors. Hard on his heels is the gang, who are hunting him to take hostage. Soon both he, Harry and the Contessa are captured and chained up. But the gang have underestimated the Protectors....

## 17. .....WITH A LITTLE HELP FROM MY FRIENDS

*Screenplay by Sylvia Anderson*
*Directed by Jeremy Summers*
*Guest Artists:*
*Jeremy Brett as Kahan*
*Hannah Gordon as Laura*

Harry is guarding an important president on a visit to London. But then Harry's estranged wife Laura reports that their young son has been kidnapped by the President's rival Kahan, and unless Harry shoots the President, their son will suffer. So Harry does shoot the President, in cold blood. Then the Contessa shoots Harry down. But everything turns out alright in the end - the bullets were blanks and Kahan's evil plot is foiled.

## 18. FOR THE REST OF YOUR NATURAL....

*Screenplay by Tony Barwick*
*Directed by Johnny Hough*
*Guest Artist:*
*Norman Rodway as Colin Grant*

Colin Grant, a criminally insane psychopath once convicted of the murder of a little girl on the evidence of the Contessa, escapes from imprisonment. He captures the Contessa, and puts her on trial for her life... with a grotesque jury of cut-out cardboard characters headed by a teddy bear foreman. As Paul and Suki search for her, the Contessa makes her own attempt to escape. But the only way she can do this is by trying to negotiate with the crazed mind of the killer who is acting as her prosecutor.

## 19. THE BODYGUARDS

*Screenplay by Dennis Spooner*
*Directed by Don Chaffey*
*Guest Artists:*
*Freddie Jones as Robard*
*Manning Redwood as Mason*

The Protectors are hired to guard the body of a dead man - and pretend he's alive! The reason is that the dead man, Ralph Corder, was a bank robber, and the police want to catch two members of his gang, Robard and Mason, who believe he's still alive. In trying to find Corder, the two crooks give their whereabouts away, and with the assistance of the Protectors, the police arrest them and recover the stolen money.

## 20. TALKDOWN

*Screenplay by Pat and Jesse Lasky*
*Directed by Jeremy Summers*
*Guest Artist: Derren Nesbitt as Foster*

A mentally unbalanced criminal named Foster kidnaps Harry and takes him skyward in a small plane. It's all part of a bizarre plot to have Harry convicted of Foster's murder. When Foster parachutes out of the plane, Harry is left at the controls - but he doesn't know how to pilot a plane! It is up to the Contessa and Paul, on the ground, to convey the necessary information about flying to Harry by radio so that he can land the plane - he must be talked down!

## 21. A CASE FOR THE RIGHT

*Screenplay by Jesse and Pat Lasky*
*Directed by Michael Lindsay-Hogg*
*Guest Artist: Milo O'Shea as Carpiano*

After a mission that ended almost fatally for Harry when he was handcuffed to a briefcase with a bomb in it, he and the Contessa decide to investigate. The trail leads them to the home of an Italian Prince, Carpiano, then to an old Roman tomb where the Prince is holding a party. Gatecrashing the party, they discover a sinister plot which must be frustrated - the Prince is head of a neo-Fascist organisation which is about to become violently active!

## 22. A MATTER OF LIFE AND DEATH

*Screenplay by Donald James*
*Directed by Don Chaffey*

A dozen hippies have died in similar hit-and-run accidents, and they were all working for a man named Goran. Harry tracks down the man, but before he can reveal anything but a confusing clue, Goran is shot dead. The skills of the Protectors soon unravel Goran's clue, and they discover an elaborate smuggling operation. All the pieces of the puzzle begin to fit when they discover the unusual nature of the contraband involved - blood plasma!

## 23. IT COULD BE PRACTICALLY ANYWHERE ON THE ISLAND

*Screenplay by Tony Barwick*
*Directed by Robert Vaughn*
*Guest Artists:*
*Sherwood Price as Felix Costa*
*Linda Staab as Linda McCall*

It seems that Harry's latest mission, to set up a hotel detective's office, would be simple. But when Linda McCall, a rich and beautiful guest at the hotel, has her dog Muffin stolen from her, it becomes more serious than Harry could possibly have imagined. The truth is that Muffin has been stolen to smuggle microfilmed secrets of a new atomic power station. However, when the dog is finally found, the plot has been foiled by Muffin who has accidentally eaten the microfilm!

## 24. VOCAL

*Screenplay by Brian Clemens*
*Directed by Cyril Frankel*
*Guest Artists:*
*David Buck as Azon*
*Ian Hogg as Gregg*
*Shane Rimmer as Vickers*

When Harry goes abroad, three vengeful criminals, Gregg, Vickers and John Azon, go to work on the rest of the Protectors' London office. Vickers is an extraordinarily good voice impersonator, and by using 'Harry's' voice over the telephone, he lures the Contessa, Suki and a temporarily blinded Paul to

Harry's apartment and holds them prisoner there. All that the three have in their favour is that Suki has a knife.

## 25. IT WAS ALL OVER IN LEIPZIG

*Screenplay by Donald James*
*Directed by Don Chaffey*
*Guest Artist:*
*Ron Randell as Jim Palmer*

While investigating a plot to overthrow a Mediterranean island government, the Contessa meets up with an old flame, co-Protector Jim Palmer. Their first suspect in the planned coup is a prominent island businessman, Adam Markos. To Harry and Paul, it soon

becomes clear that Markos is innocent, and Jim Palmer himself is the man they're seeking. But the Contessa doesn't know that, and she's on a speedboat trip with Palmer.

## 26. CEREMONY FOR THE DEAD

*Screenplay by Donald James*
*Directed by Jeremy Summers*

A foreign President's wife wants her husband protected on his arrival for medical treatment. The Protectors decide to bring the President in by sea, but make it appear to all concerned that he will be arriving by air. Even this ruse doesn't work, and the President is kidnapped. But when the Protectors rescue him, he's already dead. And he's been dead all along. Now they have to question the President's wife to find out why they've been deceived and what exactly is going on.

---

## THE PROTECTORS (SERIES II)
26 episodes

## 1. BAGMAN

*Screenplay by Terry Nation*
*Directed by John Hough*
*Guest Artists:*
*Stephan Chase as Christian*
*Patricia Haines as Mrs Andersen*

The abduction of Evi Andersen is followed by a ransom demand to her mother in Copenhagen. Mrs. Andersen calls in the Protectors, who try to negotiate for Evi's release with the kidnapper, Christian Janson. But the ransom arrangements fall through, and Janson becomes the target in a desperate game of hunt-the-criminal which has its climax in a disused fort.

## 2. THE BRIDGE

*Screenplay by Tony Barwick*
*Directed by Jeremy Summers*
*Guest Artists:*
*Richard Morant as David Mitchell*
*Michael Goodliffe as De Santos*
*James Maxwell as Mitchell*

An innocent girl is abducted by a misplaced idealist, David Mitchell, who is the son of her father's best friend. The price for her return: explosives and someone who knows how to handle them. Harry masquerades as the

explosives expert in order to foil David's plan to kill a special American government envoy in a bomb attack.

## 3. FIGHTING FUND

*Screenplay by John Kruse*
*Directed by Jeremy Summers*
*Guest Artist:*
*Lisa Daniely as Marquesa Visconti*

A gang of terrorists steal a valuable art collection and arrange an auction for secretive, private collectors. Harry is determined to sabotage the sale, so that the terrorists will not be able to raise money to continue their operations. Using the Contessa as a buyer at the telephone auction, he unearths a trail of clues that will lead to the terrorists' secret headquarters.

## 4. QUIN

*Screenplay by Trevor Preston*
*Directed by Don Leaver*
*Guest Artist: Peter Vaughan as Quin*

The most influential and feared man in the international mercenary world is Quin, and his vicious reign of terror must be brought to an end. The search for this ruthless man takes the Protectors to Spain, where Harry poses as a client requiring Quin's services. But Quin wants a demonstration of Harry's authenticity; he wants Harry to

kill someone in his cause.... and that person turns out to be the Contessa! Harry must think fast if the Protectors are to survive.

## 5. LENA

*Screenplay by Trevor Preston*
*Directed by Don Leaver*
*Guest Artist: Judy Parfitt as Lena*

A female journalist, Lena Haydon, is convinced that Mauro Carpiano, a ruthless Italian politician, has been involved in the murder of his own father, in order to gain an inheritance. When she involves the Protectors in the case, it becomes a search for a friend of the dead man who is hiding. Harry is convinced that this friend knows the truth, and when he reveals all, it will make a sensational newspaper exposé for Lena.

## 6. GOODBYE GEORGE

*Screenplay by Brian Clemens*
*Directed by Michael Lindsay-Hogg*
*Guest Artists:*
*Paul Jones as Caspar*
*Geraldine Moffatt as Maria*

Millionaire Cedric Parton wants to know what his son Caspar is up to in Venice. When the Contessa arrives there, she discovers that Caspar has got involved with a very strange pair named

Maria and George, to whom he is giving money for charity. But the Contessa can see that George is a con-man, the charity a fake... then George disappears - and there's a surprising climax in store for the Contessa when she confronts Caspar, who claims to have killed George!

## 7. IMPLICADO

*Screenplay by Tony Barwick*
*Directed by Jeremy Summers*
*Guest Artists:*
*Patrick Mower as Raphael Santana*
*Peter Firth as Stephen Douglas*

When the Protectors investigate the case of Stephen Douglas, an English boy arrested in Spain on drug smuggling charges, they decide he cannot be guilty. A convoluted series of leads takes them to Raphael Santana, the malicious crook behind the smuggling. Now all they have to do is <u>prove</u> Douglas's innocence and Santana's deception.

## 8. THE LAST FRONTIER

*Screenplay by Tony Barwick*
*Directed by Charles Crichton*
*Guest Artists:*
*Hildegard Neil as Irina Gayevska*
*William Lucas as Eastbrook*

Irina Gayevska, a beautiful Russian scientist who is an expert in genetics and radiation, falls in love with Eastbrook, a British Member of Parliament. But when the Protectors smuggle Irina into England to marry Eastbrook, it becomes clear that his motives are more than just romantic. But if she agrees to his wishes for her to work for the British government, it will put her life in great danger.

## 9. BAUBLES, BANGLES AND BEADS

*Screenplay by Terry Nation*
*Directed by Jeremy Summers*
*Guest Artists:*
*Federick Jaegar as Bergen*
*Yvonne Antrobus as Katie Bergen*

After the hijacking of a valuable collection of jewels, Harry and the Contessa go to Denmark. But Bergen, one of the gang who stole the jewels, has double-crossed his fellow thieves, and wants to sell back the jewels to ensure a good future for his daughter Katie. But he has been badly injured, and it will be a race between the Protectors and the other members of the gang to find Bergen alive and get the jewels.

## 10. PETARD

*Screenplay by Tony Barwick*
*Directed by Cyril Frankel*
*Guest Artists:*
*Iain Cuthbertson as Wyatt*
*Cyril Luckham as Alec Weston*

Espionage is not confined to spying amongst nations, and it is industrial espionage that draws the Protectors to the vast international IMA company. IMA's chairman, Wyatt, is extremely concerned because the company's secrets are being leaked to rivals. It is up to Harry, the Contessa and Paul to

find out which of the company's directors is responsible, and end the leaks once and for all.

## 11. BURNING BUSH

*Screenplay by Trevor Preston*
*Directed by Don Leaver*
*Guest Artist:*
*Sinead Cusack as Anne Ferris*

When Canadian heiress Anne Ferris disappears from London, her father, millionaire industrialist Adam Ferris, sends Harry to search for her. He finds her in a sectarian religious community which combines Christianity with spiritualism. And when a mentally deranged member of the community named Jenner attempts to kill them both, strange things happen that Harry is later quite unable to explain.

## 12. BORDER LINE

*Screenplay by Anthony Terpiloff*
*Directed by Charles Crichton.*
*Guest Artists:*
*Georgia Brown as Ilona Tabori*
*Oscar Homolka as Zoltan Kolas*

Janos Tabori, Hungarian patriot and freedom fighter, had to flee his country after its abortive uprising. But now he is dead, and his daughter Ilona wants him buried in his home country. Unfortunately, this means his body will have to be smuggled into Hungary, and this is where the Protectors come in. It won't be an easy job, and discovery of their operation seems certain.

## 13. WAM (Part One)

*Screenplay by Tony Barwick*
*Directed by Jeremy Summers*
*Guest Artists:*
*Prentis Hancock as*
*William Arthur McKay*
*Jill Townsend as Monica Davies*

Monica Davies, who has been cut off by her rich father, writes to him to say that she will soon be rich independently of him. When the Protectors begin following Monica in Salzburg, they soon find evidence of some sort of plot. Then

a full cable car and the telephone system at the top of a mountain are sabotaged....

## 14. WAM (Part Two)

*Credits as 13*

Inside the cable car, the holiday-makers who are now being held to a $100,000 ransom know nothing of the danger they are in. All seems to be going according to plan for Monica and her confederate Wolf: they get the money, the cable car is saved.... and it is then that the Protectors swoop on the couple.

## 15. DRAGON CHASE

*Screenplay by John Kruse*
*Directed by Charles Crichton*
*Guest Artist:*
*Donald Houston as Lockier*

Publisher Lockier has smuggled Russian Nobel prize-winning author Nickolai into Britain. But when Lockier goes away, leaving Harry to protect the dissident, disaster strikes. Lockier's son Peter, who is mixed up with a group of fanatics at his University, arranges to kidnap Nickolai. It will be a race against time for the Protectors to find Nickolai before he's smuggled out of the country.

## 16. ZEKE'S BLUES

*Screenplay Shane Rimmer*
*Directed by Jeremy Summers*
*Guest Artists:*
*Shane Rimmer as Zeke*
*Paul Curran as Kasankas*

When Harry and the Contessa encounter Zeke Daley, an old friend of Harry's from college days, Zeke invites them to a nightclub where he is the pianist. But after going there, Harry unknowingly

leads the club's owner, former underworld boss Kasankas, to a man who could incriminate Kasankas. Now only Zeke's friendship, and the Contessa, can help the trapped Harry.

## 17. DECOY

*Screenplay by Brian Clemens*
*Directed by Michael Lindsay-Hogg*
*Guest Artists:*
*Ronald Radd as Jerry Butler*
*Mark Damon as Nick Archer*

Nick Archer, a man believed to have been killed in a car explosion during a million pound diamond raid, is actually alive. When this fact is discovered by insurance agent Jerry Butler, he is murdered. When Harry comes to the scene, he too is shot and left for dead. But he escapes alive, and with the Contessa, begins to search for Archer.

## 18. A POCKETFUL OF POSIES

*Screenplay by Terry Nation*
*Directed by Cyril Frankel.*
*Guest Star:*
*Eartha Kitt as Carrie Blaine*
*Guest Artist:*
*Kieron Moore as Mario Toza*

To Carrie Blaine, an international singing star, the world is becoming frighteningly strange, and she wonders if her mind is going. Inexplicable incidents occur, such as an unpowered radio suddenly switching itself on. At first Harry intends to dismiss the case as that of a mentally unbalanced woman, but when he discovers her coffee has been laced with sedatives, he decides to investigate further.

## 19. SHADBOLT

*Screenplay by Tony Barwick*
*Directed by John Hough*
*Guest Artists:*
*Tom Bell as Shadbolt*
*Georgina Hale as Girl*

Shadbolt, a cold, calculating professional assassin, is hired to kill a man on board a train. When on the train, he ensures that he makes a strong

impression on a particular girl in order to create an alibi for himself, and then appears to the girl to leave the train. But in fact he is still aboard, waiting to kill somebody - and the somebody who will have to look out for himself is none other than Harry Rule!

## 20. SUGAR AND SPICE

*Screenplay by David Butler*
*Directed by Charles Crichton*
*Guest Artist:*
*Debbie Russ as Vicky Standish.*

A group of businessmen, determined to prevent a series of mergers that would benefit Sir Charles Standish, threaten the life of his daughter Vicky. So Harry, Paul and the Contessa are engaged by Sir Charles to take Vicky from school on a sudden history field trip. But even at a lonely farmhouse, the Protectors do not escape the dastardly manipulations of the cartel of ruthless businessmen!

## 21. BLOCKBUSTER

*Screenplay by Shane Rimmer*
*Directed by Jeremy Summers*
*Guest Artists:*
*Peter Jeffrey as Police Inspector*
*Christopher Neame as Bailey*
*Stanley Meadows as Birch*

The head of a security firm asks the Protectors to help after he has been the victim of three seemingly impossible platinum robberies. In the last robbery, a police cordon was thrown up immediately after the security van had been hi-jacked - but no trace of it was ever found. Suspicions are cast on a local scrapyard owner named Bailey, but it's going to be tough proving anything.

## 22. WHEELS

*Screenplay by Tony Barwick*
*Directed by David Tomblim*

A man named Manning has stolen details of some numbered Swiss bank accounts, and is keeping them in a briefcase in his safe, holding them to ransom. In an effort to expose the insider in the bank who must be helping

Manning, Harry cracks the safe and swaps the briefcase for an identical, empty one. After notifying the bank of its contents, Harry now has to return the case, without alerting Manning and the insider that their game is up. This involves arranging an elaborate car crash between Manning's limousine, a rally car containing Paul and Harry, and the Contessa in a following car!

## 23. THE TIGER AND THE GOAT

*Screenplay by Trevor Preston*
*Directed by Jeremy Summers*
*Guest Artists:*
*Douglas Wilmer as*
*Commander Whiting*
*Derek Godfrey as David Barsella*

A man who calls himself Commander Whiting from British Intelligence comes to the Contessa Caroline and asks her to provide a safe place for a man she once loved named Barsella. Whiting says that an assassin is looking for the Contessa's old flame. But when Barsella arrives to stay in her house, the Contessa realises that she is the goat that has been used by the hunter to lure the tiger into his sights - and the hunter is Whiting!

## 24. THE INSIDER

*Screenplay by Trevor Preston*
*Directed by Don Leaver*
*Guest Artist: Stuart Wilson as Smith*

The master negative of a film is stolen and all the prints destroyed only seven weeks before the premiere. The producer and the Protectors soon meet a man named Smith who has stolen the film and is prepared to sell it back. A deal is arranged, and Smith is carefully watched. But when it is discovered that he does not leave the producer's office building after meetings, the Protectors

decide it must be an inside job. Then the Contessa sees the thief on the roof of the building. It proves to be a macabre, danger-laden chase to catch him.

## 25. TRIAL

*Screenplay by Robert Banks Stewart*
*Directed by Charles Crichton*
*Guest Artists:*
*Joss Ackland as Arthur Gordon*
*Gwen Cherrell as Anne Gordon*
*Richard Hurndall as Justice Cronin*

When his son John is put on trial for murder, Arthur Gordon, already suffering from a nervous breakdown, begins to interfere with the course of justice. After Gordon's wife Anne goes to the Protectors, Harry soon discovers that Arthur Gordon is planning to assassinate the judge of his son's case, Justice Cronin. He must be stopped...

## 26. ROUTE 27

*Screenplay by Terry Nation*
*Directed by Don Leaver*
*Guest Artist: Michael Coles as Sandven*

The father of an eighteen-year-old heroin overdose victim engages Harry to smash the gang responsible for his son's death. But things go wrong and soon the tables are turned and the drug gang are looking for Harry. He knows where their mislaid drug consignment is, and they want that information so badly that they kidnap the Contessa and will release her only if Harry reveals it. But when he does, and they've released the Contessa, they still want to kill Harry.

---

**Principal Credits**

52 thirty minute episodes
Colour
A Group Three Production for ITC
World Wide Distribution
Produced by Gerry Anderson and
Reg Hill
Created by Lew Grade
Music composed and directed by
John Cameron
Theme 'Avenues and Alleyways' by
Mitch Murray and Peter Callander

1975

1999: Man has conquered the surface of the Moon, and has established a fully staffed, self-supporting Moonbase, named Alpha, where scientific experiments are conducted and data about space gathered.

But on the reverse side of the moon, man has been dumping nuclear waste in special disposal areas. And when an explosion is somehow triggered from space in one of those areas, a chain reaction begins, spreading throughout the entire disposal site.

Nuclear explosions soon follow, and eventually the sheer size of the explosions tear the Moon out of its orbit around Earth, and send it spinning into space.

On Moonbase Alpha, the crew of approximately three hundred survives. Travelling through space on the rogue Moon, they are destined for the greatest adventures of their lives, encountering strange new worlds and alien life forms.

## Major characters

COMMANDER JOHN KOENIG - the Commander of Moonbase Alpha, now responsible for the future of the entire crew
DR HELENA RUSSELL - chief of Alpha's Medical Section, widowed, with a strong attachment to John Koenig
PROFESSOR BERGMAN - a brilliant scientist, handicapped only by an artificial heart which reduces the speed of his emotional responses
ALAN CARTER - the chief space pilot who often accompanies Koenig on off-moon trips
PAUL MORROW- Koenig's second-in-command

## Cast

Commander John Koenig...
Martin Landau
Dr Helena Russell...Barbara Bain
Professor Bergman...Barry Morse
Alan Carter...Nick Tate
Paul Morrow...Prentis Hancock
Dr Mathias...Anton Philips
David Kano...Clifton Jones
Sandra Benes...Zienia Merton
Tanya...Suzanne Roquette

## 1. BREAKAWAY

*Screenplay by George Bellak*
*Directed by Lee Katzin*
*Guest Artist: Roy Dotrice as*
*Commissioner Simmonds*

John Koenig is at Moonbase Alpha to supervise a deep space probe that will explore the rogue planet Meta, from which there are signs of an advanced form of life. But on the other side of the Moon, at a disposal area where all Earth's nuclear waste is dumped, there is an accident. There is a nuclear explosion, gravity control is affected, and the Moon is pulled out of orbit, moving inexorably away from Earth. Koenig takes a decision that the entire crew should stay on Moonbase Alpha - because to evacuate and attempt a return to Earth would be suicidal.

## 2. MATTER OF LIFE AND DEATH

*Screenplay by Art Wallace and*
*Johnny Byrne*
*Directed by Charles Crichton*
*Guest Artist: Richard Johnson as Lee*

Helena's husband Lee, who was previously missing presumed dead, suddenly turns up on an Alphan spacecraft probing the planet Terra Nova, which is apparently capable of sustaining human life. But when the spacecraft returns to Alpha, Lee warns them not to go near the planet, and then dies. Koenig, thinking of re-locating his entire crew to this Earth-like planet, takes an advance party to its surface. Then Koenig is killed, Lee re-appears

with another warning, and Koenig comes back to life. He must now decide - should he order an exodus to this strange new planet?

## 3. THE INFERNAL MACHINE

*Screenplay by Anthony Terpiloff and*
*Elizabeth Barrows*
*Directed by David Tomblin*
*Guest Star: Leo McKern as Companion*

A huge spacecraft, breaking every known law of aerospace propulsion, appears in the sky and is given permission to land on the Moon. Koenig, Helena and Bergman are admitted to the craft, where they meet an extraordinarily ancient man, Companion. He explains that the whole craft is a living machine named Gwent, which he serves. But Companion is sick and soon dies. Gwent, also, is weakening, and when it demands that Koenig and Helena act as replacements for Companion, they launch a grim battle of wits against this machine with a human personality.

## 4. DRAGON'S DOMAIN

*Screenplay by Christopher Penfold*
*Directed by Charles Crichton*
*Guest Star:*
*Gianni Garko as Tony Cellini*

Tony Cellini and Koenig are old friends. But when the Moon drifts close to an area near the planet Ultra where Cellini survived an incredible experience, he appears to go berserk, and attempts to

take off, entirely alone, in an Eagle command module. It was once on his way to Ultra that Cellini and three others came to an eerie graveyard of spaceships. They were attacked by a monster, a gruesome, rampaging mass of writhing tentacles, and only Cellini survived to tell the tale. Now back in the same area of space, Cellini wants to vindicate himself.

## 5. THE TESTAMENT OF ARKADIA

*Screenplay by Johnny Byrne*
*Directed by David Tomblin*
*Guest Stars:*
*Orsa Maria Guerrini as Luke Ferro*
*Lisa Harrow as Anna Davis*

When the Moon comes close to the planet Arkadia, it stops moving and power begins to drop dangerously. Koenig decides to visit the planet, and takes Helena, Bergman, Alan Carter, and specialists Luke Ferro and Anna Davis with him. In a cave, they find human skeletons and inscriptions on the wall which Davis and Ferro translate, and a strange story is revealed . A holocaust struck Arkadia a long, long time ago - and the survivors who migrated to another planet became the original humans of Earth! As suddenly as it began, the power loss on the Moon ceases and Koenig decides to leave the empty, but once again, habitable, Arkadia. However, Luke and Anna have fallen in love, and by tricking Koenig, remain on Arkadia to make it their own Eden.

## 6. THE LAST ENEMY

*Screenplay by Bob Kellett*
*Directed by Bob Kellett*
*Guest Artist:*
*Caroline Mortimer as Dione*

Moonbase Alpha becomes caught up in a war between two planets when a spacecraft uses the Moon as a base to attack its enemy. The spacecraft is destroyed and a single survivor goes to Alpha in an escape capsule. It is a young and beautiful girl named Dione, from the planet Betha, who explains that her planet is, and always has been, at war with the planet Delta. Koenig contacts the Supreme Commander of Delta Armed Forces and the Chief Commissioner of Betha Defence to negotiate a ceasefire. But he has reckoned without the cunning of fervent Dione.

## 7. MISSION OF THE DARIANS

*Screenplay by Johnny Byrne*
*Directed by Ray Austin*
*Guest Star: Joan Collins as Kara*
*Guest Artist:*
*Dennis Burgess as Neman*

Decoded signals from a colossal, fifty-mile-long spaceship indicate a major emergency. Koenig orders a mercy flight to the spaceship, taking with him, Helena, Bergman, Alan Carter, Paul Morrow and a security man. They discover that the ship is commanded by

agelessly beautiful Kara and a man named Neman, who, along with twelve other people, are the only true survivors of a planet called Daria that they left 900 years before. But when Koenig discovers that the Darians have been keeping themselves alive by cannibalistically transplanting organs from a degenerate civilisation in another part of the spaceship, he realises that he and his team must act quickly if they are to avoid meeting the same fate.

## 8. THE TROUBLED SPIRIT

*Screenplay by Johnny Byrne*
*Directed by Ray Austin*
*Guest Artists:*
*Giancarlo Prette as Dan Mateo*
*Hilary Dwyer as Laura Adams*
*Anthony Nicholls as Dr James Warren*

Dan Mateo, a botanist conducting experiments in the Hydroponic Unit with his assistant Laura Adams, suddenly collapses. Then, under Helena's care in the Medical Unit, he sees the shadowy shape of a horribly scarred man. Helena also sees it, believing it to resemble Mateo. When Koenig and Dr Warren, head of the Hydroponic Unit, forbid Mateo to continue his experiments, Warren sees the shadowy figure - and then dies. When Mateo secretly continues his experiments, Laura Adams quarrels with him. Again the mysterious figure appears - and Laura dies. On Bergman's advice, Mateo is allowed to carry out his experiments openly. Once again, the

ghostly, mutilated figure emerges, and it is without doubt a spirit Mateo. Now some form of scientific exorcism may be the only hope.

## 9. SPACE BRAIN

*Screenplay by Christopher Penfold*
*Directed by Charles Crichton*
*Guest Artist: Shane Rimmer as Kelly*

The sudden outburst of strange, alien hieroglyphics on all of Alpha's screens is followed by the sighting of what looks like a huge space anemone. An Eagle sent to investigate is horribly compressed and propelled back towards Alpha as a white-hot missile. Then Alan Carter's colleague, Kelly, space-walking on another Eagle, comes into contact with the anemone-like being. Back on Alpha, it is clear that Kelly has been taken over and possessed by the mysterious alien force. By the time that Kelly is able to communicate that the huge space 'brain' is not aggressive, but just trying to prevent a collision, it may be too late. Koenig has ordered an Eagle loaded with an enormous nuclear charge to be aimed at the creature!

## 10. WAR GAMES

*Screenplay by Christopher Penfold*
*Directed by Charles Crichton*
*Guest Star:*
*Anthony Valentine as the Male Alien*
*Guest Artist:*
*Isla Blair as the Female Alien*

Moonbase Alpha is at war, attacked by an un-named planet. Windows are smashed and men sucked into space. Defending Eagles are destroyed in the air. Main Mission is wrecked and 129 are dead. Only one hope remains - to confront the enemy, so Koenig and Helena set out in an unarmed Eagle. They meet eerie figures silhouetted in strange columns of light - a male and a female alien. The aliens explain that they are protecting them from Earthmen's fear - an enemy which they claim would destroy their civilisation. Then they negate the whole war, leaving Alpha as it was before but with Koenig warned, their planet safe.

## 11. END OF ETERNITY

*Screenplay by Johnny Byrne*
*Directed by Ray Austin*
*Guest Artist: Peter Bowles as Balor*

The appearance of an asteroid, three light years from the nearest star, that must have been travelling for a thousand years in space, is baffling. When the computer reports there is an atmosphere source somewhere inside it, Koenig and two others land on the asteroid. In the living chamber inside, they find an unconscious, terribly injured humanoid alien. But when he is taken to Moonbase, there is not a scratch on him. The man gives his name as Balor, citizen of the planet Progron. He is a scientist who discovered immortality, and has been blamed for the ensuing meaninglessness Progron's people felt in their lives, and imprisoned in a living rock and cast into space. When Koenig realises that the immortal, re-generating man is a complete psychopath, he knows he must kill him. Koenig must lure him into an airlock and release him into space forever, but to trap him Koenig has to be with him.

## 12. THE FULL CIRCLE

*Screenplay by Jesse Lasky Jr and Pat Silver*
*Directed by Bob Kellett*

A landing party is sent to the newly discovered planet Retha. But when they don't return, a full-scale rescue is led by Koenig. Alan Carter and Sandra are separated from the rest of the rescue team, and they stumble across a caveman-like civilisation, led by the Cave Chief and his Cave Wife, who strangely resemble Koenig and Helena. It soon becomes clear that there is a time warp on the planet and that some of the crew will have to be brought back from 40,000 years of history into the present!

## 13. DEATH'S OTHER DOMINION

*Screenplay by Anthony Terpiloff and Elizabeth Barrows*
*Directed by Charles Crichton*
*Guest Star: Brian Blessed as Cabot Rowland.*
*Guest Artist: John Shrapnell as Captain Jack Tanner*

When the Alphans are invited to share a lost paradise - and immortality- on the frozen planet, Ultima Thule, they soon discover their hosts are members of a space expedition launched from Earth in 1986. It could mean doom for them all!

## 14. COLLISION COURSE

*Screenplay by Anthony Terpiloff*
*Directed by Ray Austin*
*Special Guest Star: Margaret Leighton as Arra*

The Moon is on a collision course with a planet many times its size, and a decision to change the course of the planet, by laying nuclear mines in its path, is postponed when it is discovered that the planet may harbour life. Koenig immediately sets out to reconnoitre the planet, but it is intercepted by the spaceship of Arra, Queen of the planet, which is called Astheria. She wants Koenig to call off the nuclear mines operation. But on Moonbase, they are convinced it is the only way to prevent a collision. Koenig must return to Moonbase to argue the case for Arra. But Helena diagnoses that he has radiation sickness and is hallucinating. What is to be done, with time fast running out?

## 15. VOYAGER'S RETURN

*Screenplay by Johnny Byrne*
*Directed by Bob Kellett*
*Guest Star: Jeremy Kemp as Dr Ernst Linden*
*Guest Artist: Barry Stokes as Jim Haines*

Moonbase Alpha receives signals from the computer of Voyager One, an unmanned spaceship launched in 1985. But since its launch, Voyager One's Queller Drive engine has been polluting space with dangerous fast neutrons that annihilate matter. There is only man aboard, Dr Ernst Linden, who could possibly shut down the Queller drive. It will be a desperate race against time. But Linden's assistant, Jim Haines, whose parents died because of the Queller drive malfunction, discovers that Linden is in fact the inventor of the drive, having changed his name from Ernst Queller. He loses his temper , and hits Linden/Queller. But Helena revives the injured man, and he finishes the task of disabling the destructive drive. But then a humanoid alien with a force of three spaceships arrives, seeking vengeance for the millions of his fellow citizens killed by the effects of the Queller drive...

## 16. ALPHA CHILD

*Screenplay by Christopher Penfold*
*Directed by Ray Austin*
*Guest Artists:*
*Julian Glover as Jarak*
*Cyd Hayman as Cynthia Crawford*

Cynthia Crawford gives birth to Alpha's first baby, and names the boy Jackie. But within hours the baby grows into a man who calls himself Jarak. He says that he is one of 120 travellers escaping from their planet, because they were outcasts of a system of ruthlessly imposed genetic conformity. Their plan is to take over the bodies of those on Moonbase. Jarak explains that the moments of human birth and death are ideally suited to this purpose. Then suddenly, six spaceships appear from Jarak's home planet to confront him and his band of runaways... the outcome will determine the fate of Moonbase Alpha and its crew.

## 17. THE LAST SUNSET

*Screenplay by Christopher Penfold*
*Directed by Charles Crichton*

The prospect of a normal life dangles tantalizingly for the occupants of the runaway Moon when they find a new solar system with a potentially habitable planet that Bergman identifies as Ariel.

For a while, the crew are able to experience real air, warm sunshine and the hope of a new Earth. Paul Morrow and Sandra Benes contemplate the possibility of a normal, loving, Earth-bound relationship. But some strange discoveries on the surface of the planet soon shatter all the dreams of the future.

## 18. FORCE OF LIFE

*Screenplay by Johnny Byrne*
*Directed by David Tomblin*
*Guest Star:*
*Ian McShane as Anton Zoref*
*Guest Artist:*
*Gay Hamilton as Eva Zoref*

After the appearance of a strange ball of blue light in the sky, technician Anton Zoref collapses, unconscious. And when he recovers, he becomes possessed with a terrifying need for heat. Everything he touches - machinery, people - freezes instantly. Koenig orders power supplies to be shut off, and Zoref begins seeking human bodies for heat! His wife Eva is only saved by Alan Carter's quick thinking. But when Carter shoots Zoref, the laser energy gives him huge strength, and he breaks into the ship's reactor. A massive fission explosion occurs, from which a swirling comet of blue light heads out into the space sky.

## 19. GUARDIAN OF PIRI

*Screenplay by Christopher Penfold*
*Directed by Charles Crichton*
*Guest Artist:*
*Catherine Schell as the Pirian*

Three Alphans disappear while investigating the beautiful planet Piri. With Alan Carter, Koenig lands on the planet, where he finds the three men, entranced with ecstatic smiles on their faces. Suddenly, an incredibly beautiful woman appears from within a brilliant light and explains that she is the servant of the Guardian of Piri. She offers the entire population of the Moon the opportunity to give up their human pain and enjoy Pirian life, as the first three Alphans had done. But only Koenig realises that she is offering them all a living death, and a terrible conflict ensues.

## 20. MISSING LINK

*Screenplay by Edward Di Lorenzo*
*Directed by Ray Austin*
*Guest Artist: Joanna Dunham as Vana*
*Special Guest Star:*
*Peter Cushing as Raan*

When Koenig is severely injured in an Eagle crash, Dr Russell battles to save him. But inside his head, Koenig is fighting a different battle. He believes himself to be on the planet Zenno, where a scientist named Raan is using him as an anthropological specimen. When Koenig becomes involved with Raan's beautiful daughter Vana, he must fight against his desire to stay on the planet Zenno or he may never survive to live again on Moonbase.

## 21. ANOTHER TIME, ANOTHER PLACE

*Screenplay by Johnny Byrne*
*Directed by David Tomblin*
*Guest Artist: Judy Geeson as Regina Kesslann*

It is a nightmare experience for the Moonbase personnel and for Regina Kesslann in particular when the Moon is caught in a strange vortex and produces a duplicate of itself. Regina begins to see the future... in which Moonbase once again meets its double, and finds it destroyed. Inexorably, it begins to happen.

## 22. EARTHBOUND

*Screenplay by Anthony Terpiloff*
*Directed by Charles Crichton*
*Guest Artist: Roy Dotrice as Commissioner Simmonds*
*Special Guest Star: Christopher Lee as Captain Zantor*

A spaceship makes a crash landing on the Moon. On board, Captain Zantor and four other tall, striking aliens are found. Zantor explains that they left their dying planet, Kaldor, to find Earth. Commissioner Simmonds believes that the Kaldorians represent an opportunity to once again find Earth; they have one space on their craft and Simmonds is determined to have it. Koenig insists that the computer choose the most appropriate Alphan to join the five Kaldorians on their mission, but Simmonds becomes desperate to have the place.

## 23. RING AROUND THE MOON

*Screenplay by Edward Di Lorenzo*
*Directed by Ray Austin*

Moonbase Alpha is taken captive by a huge energy sphere from the planet Triton. The sphere was a probe mission to discover if Earth would be threatening to the planet Triton. But since its launch Triton has blown up and disintegrated two million miles away. When the probe takes over Helena to use her as a communicator with the Earth people, it is their task to attempt to prove that Triton <u>has</u> been destroyed and that therefore Alpha cannot be a threat...

## 24. THE BLACK SUN

*Screenplay by David Weir*
*Directed by Lee Katzin*
*Guest Artist: Paul Jones as Ryan*

The Moon is heading into a black sun. It's huge, it has a tremendous gravitational attraction, and it pulls everything into itself, even light. Koenig decides that six people in an Eagle might hold better chances of survival than those on Alpha. Helena is one of the six who are assembled in the team that is sent away from the Moon. Koenig stays on the Moonbase, which is drawn into the black mass. And though, after a strange, cosmic experience, those on Moonbase survive, they are still separated from the others, but where is the Eagle with Helena and the five other specially chosen occupants?

## New major characters

MAYA - rescued from her own planet, this sexy, female alien with shape-changing powers became Alpha's Science Officer.
TONY VERDESCHI - the security chief with a sense of humour, who just might be falling for Maya...

## Cast

Commander Koenig....Martin Landau
Dr Helena Russell.....Barbara Bain
Maya.....Catherine Schell
Tony Verdeschi.....Tony Anholt
Alan Carter.....Nick Tate
Sahn.....Zienia Merton
Dr Matthias.....Anton Phillips
Yasko.....Yasuko Nagazumi
Fraser.....John Hug

## 1. THE METAMORPH

*Screenplay by Johnny Byrne*
*Directed by Charles Crichton*
*With Brian Blessed as Mentor*
*Catherine Schell as Maya*

On the trail of two captured pilots, Koenig goes to the planet Psychon to rescue them. On the planet, he finds Mentor, a man lording over a world of virtual zombies who work for him as miners. Mentor believes that, using a biological computer that feeds on the minds and bodies of his slaves, he can rebuild Psychon as the beautiful world it once was. But he needs more human fodder - the Alphans! By using Mentor's daughter Maya, who has the power of molecular transformation - she is a shape-changer - Koenig believes he can defeat Mentor. Maya is unaware of her father's psychopathic ruthlessness, and this ignorance is to Koenig's advantage. Finally, the Alphans escape, and Maya with them. Her powers and remarkable scientific knowledge will be welcome on the wayward Moon....

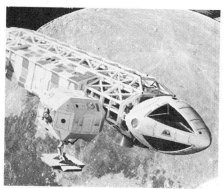

## 2. THE EXILES

*Screenplay by Donald James*
*Directed by Ray Austin*
*With Peter Duncan as Cantar*
*Stacy Dorning as Zova*

Trailing through space are fifty cylinder-shaped objects. When Koenig recovers one, they find inside a young man named Cantar. He appeals to Koenig to save his friends from their cylinders claiming they have all been usurped from their home planet by invaders. But when Koenig recovers Cantar's wife Zova from her cylinder, trouble begins. The two force their way into Alpha's power section and use its energy to transport them, with Helena and Tony as hostages, to their home planet, from which they were in fact exiled for crimes against their own people. But 300 years have passed, and this means there is one chance for the two Alphans to save themselves...

## 3. JOURNEY TO WHERE

*Screenplay by Donald James*
*Directed by Tom Clegg*
*With Freddie Jones as Dr Logan*
*Isla Blair as Carla*

Hopes are high when a message is received by neutrone transmission from Earth. But though the Moon has been in outer space for only a few months, it is 2120 AD on Earth. The message comes from a Texan space scientist named Dr Charles Logan, who explains to the Alphans some technology which will give them one opportunity to return to Earth. Koenig decides that he, Helena and Alan Carter will test it out before returning the entire crew to Earth. This cautious move is proven very wise when somehow the three of them arrive on Earth in 1339, in Scotland, which is engaged in a civil war with England!

## 4. ONE MOMENT OF HUMANITY

*Screenplay by Tony Barwick*
*Directed by Charles Crichton*
*With Billie Whitelaw as Zamara*
*Leigh Lawson as Zarl*

A striking alien woman named Zamara materialises aboard Moonbase Alpha and takes two people - Helena and Tony - back to her planet, Vega. Zamara and her accomplice Zarl are in fact super-androids developed by successive generations of self-reproducing computers. The humans who invented the first computers still exist on Vega, and the androids want to wipe them out. Their plan in kidnapping the two Alphans is to learn the ways of aggression and killing, about which they know nothing. Zamara and Zarl begin a long and unpleasant process of antagonising Helena and Tony in an effort to gain the information they need.

## 5. ALL THAT GLISTERS

*Screenplay by Keith Miles*
*Directed by Ray Austin*
*With Patrick Mower as Dave O'Reilly*

After scanning a planet which contains Milgonite, a rare mineral vital to Alpha's life support system, the Alphans are eager to visit it. But by the time they discover that there is no Milgonite, only a deceptive lethal, living rock, it is too late. The deadly rock is already aboard Alpha, and it survives on water - which it can find in the human body! It is geologist Dave O'Reilly and Maya who devise a way to combat the menace.

## 6. THE MARK OF ARCHANON

*Screenplay by Lew Schwartz*
*Directed by Charles Crichton*
*With John Standing as Pasc*
*Michael Gallagher as Etrec*
*Veronica Lang as Lyra*

A survey reveals a metallic cabinet long-buried beneath the surface of the Moon. Inside are found Pasc and his son Etrec, from Archanon, the Planet of Peace. Pasc was part of a team sent to Earth on a mission of goodwill, but the hatred and violence on Earth was contagious, and the two affected were locked away by their own people - by Pasc's wife Lyra, in fact. But Pasc decides that this new lease of life may be his opportunity to make up for past misdeeds.

## 7. THE TAYBOR

*Screenplay by Thom Keyes*
*Directed by Bob Brooks*
*With Willoughby Goddard as Taybor*

Taybor materialises on the Moon, an interstellar trader with a wonderful spaceship, the S.S. Emporium , that travels through hyper-space. When Koenig realises that the engine on Taybor's remarkable craft could transport the Alpha personnel to any planet, even Earth, he offers the entire Moon in exchange for the secret of Taybor's hyper-spacial travel. But Taybor wants something else - Maya! When Koenig refuses such an exchange, Taybor kidnaps her.

## 8. BRIAN THE BRAIN

*Screenplay by Jack Ronder*
*Directed by Kevin Connor*
*With Bernard Cribbins as Brain*

A spaceship approaching the Moon identifies itself as one of the four 'Swift' ships that left Earth in 1996 and disappeared without a trace. Koenig is astonished when he discovers that there are no crew aboard, just a lively computer named Brian the Brain. But when he and Helena go on board the 'Swift' ship, Brian kidnaps them.

## 9. THE RULES OF LUTON

*Screenplay by Charles Woodgrove*
*Directed by Val Guest*

Temporarily left on Luton, a planet rich in vegetation, while their Eagle is repaired, Koenig and Maya cannot resist the temptation to explore. But when Koenig eats some berries and Maya picks a flower, a thunderous voice booms out accusing them of murder. Though they plead ignorance their damage to the plants is unforgivable to the Judges of the planet and they must face the consequences. The two Alphans are forced into battle against some other criminal aliens, with the promise that the survivors will gain their freedom.

## 10. NEW ADAM, NEW EVE

*Screenplay by Terence Feely*
*Directed by Charles  Crichton*
*With Guy Rolfe as Magus*

A man appears claiming to be God, selects two couples to begin a new Earth, and explains he was rather disappointed with the way the first one turned out. The couples are rather mismatched - Helena with Tony Vereschi, and Koenig with Maya - but using his powers, 'God' makes it all seem alright. But when the four Alphans discover that God is not God, but just Magus, a cosmic magician who knows the ultimate secrets of physics, they are on the path to finding his weakness and returning to Alpha.

## 11. SEED OF DESTRUCTION

*Screenplay by John Goldsmith*
*Directed by Kevin Connor*

Whilst exploring a bizarre, jewel-like asteroid, Koenig is detained and replaced by a double. The fake Koenig returns to Moonbase, and it is only slowly that the Alphans recognise that there is something strange about him. And when Maya analyses a crystal 'Koenig' has brought back from the asteroid, she is startled. The crystal is a seed which will draw all the energy from Moonbase in order to revitalise its home, the asteroid where the real Koenig is still a prisoner.

## 12. THE A-B CHRYSALIS

*Screenplay by Tony Barwick*
*Directed by Val Guest*
*With Ina Skriver as A*
*Sarah Douglas as B*

The Moon has been suffering regular twelve-hourly bombardments by enormous electrical waves, and one more such wave could spell final destruction for Moonbase Alpha. Koenig decides to go to the source of the bombardments, a nearby planet. He discovers a civilisation there whose people are in a chrysalis stage, protected

only by their computer, which sees Moonbase as a threat to them and is therefore attacking it. Then two of the people come out of the chrysalis stage into consciousness.

## 13. THE CATACOMBS OF THE MOON

*Screenplay by Anthony Terpiloff*
*Directed by Robert Lynn*
*With James Laurenson as*
*Patrick Osgood*

Down in the catacombs of the Moon, engineer Patrick Osgood is searching for titanium. It is for a dual purpose; it is needed to save his wife's life in heart surgery, and it is vital to Moonbase Alpha's life support system, and stocks of the metal are low. Time is running out, and when Osgood fails to find any titanium, he becomes very unbalanced. He forces the medical team to release his wife, and takes her into the catacombs. Koenig decides that some of the titanium in the store can be released for the operation - but now the Osgoods have to be found.

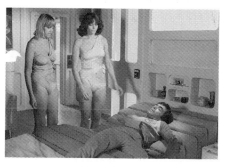

## 14. SPACE WARP

*Screenplay by Charles Woodgrove*
*Directed by Peter Medak*

Two crises strike the Alphans simultaneously. Koenig and Tony, checking out a derelict spaceship in Eagle One, encounter a space warp and end up five light years away. Meanwhile, Maya is stricken by a mysterious fever that Helena can neither diagnose nor cure. Though Koenig and Tony begin to discover a way to return through the space warp, on Alpha, Maya is deliriously changing into all sorts of creatures, and before long she changes into a space animal and escapes to the Moon's surface.

## 15. A MATTER OF BALANCE

*Screenplay by Pip and Jane Baker*
*Directed by Charles Crichton*
*With Stuart Wilson as Vindrus*
*Lynn Frederick as Shermeen*

When Koenig decides to explore an apparently lifeless planet, he takes botanist Shermeen in his landing party. In a temple on the planet into which she wanders, Shermeen comes under the spell of a being named Vindrus. She wants to help save Vindrus' doomed race - but she doesn't realise that for each of Vindrus' group that is saved, one Alphan will be doomed - and she is to be the first.

## 16. THE BETA CLOUD

*Screenplay by Charles Woodgrove*
*Directed by Robert Lynn*

After a cloud of space dust causes a mystery illness on Alpha, an Eagle crew is sent to track the storm cloud. But when the Eagle returns a week later, its only occupant is a huge, terrifying space creature. The cloud returns, and a voice explains to the Alphans that the space creature is their agent, and they want the Moonbase life support system. Tony and Maya fight a desperate battle against the seemingly indestructible creature. At one moment, when both believe their death is imminent, they confirm their love for one another.

## 17. THE LAMBDA FACTOR

*Screenplay by Terrance Dicks*
*Directed by Charles Crichton*
*With Deborah Fallender as Carolyn*

A pretty, young Alpha technician dies a horrible and unexplained death. Alan Carter is almost killed by a switched-off atomic motor. Maya discovers that a large gaseous cloud in space is giving off Lamda waves - waves that would give some people paranormal mental powers. Then a girl named Carolyn takes over the Command Centre and the whole of Moonbase, using these extraordinary powers. Koenig must fight a merciless mental battle against her that will decide the future of Moonbase and its inhabitants.

## 18. THE BRINGERS OF WONDER (PART ONE)

*Screenplays by Terence Feely*
*Directed by Tom Clegg*

After crashing his Eagle, Koenig is dragged unconscious from the blazing wreckage and hooked up to the Brain Impulse Machine. Meanwhile, a faster-than-light ship arrives on the Moon. It is the 'Superswift', a craft that was on the drawing board when the Moon broke away. Everyone in the Superswift's crew seems to be known by one Alphan or another, and one of them, Tony's brother Guido, announces that transports

will soon be coming from Earth to rescue the Alphans. But when Koenig regains consciousness, he sees not fellow Earthmen, but only hideous aliens. When the aliens discover that one of the Alphans is able to see them, they plan to kill him..

## 19. THE BRINGERS OF WONDER (PART TWO)

*Screenplay by Terence Feely*
*Directed by Tom Clegg*

Having survived, Koenig suggests to Maya that perhaps it was being connected to the Brain Machine that kept him from being deceived. After she tries it, Maya too can see the hideous aliens. Meanwhile the aliens, who consume radiation to survive, are planning to manipulate three Alphans into blowing up the Moon's nuclear waste dumps to create energy for them to live on. Soon it is left to just Koenig, Maya and Helena to defeat the devastating force of the aliens!

## 20. THE SEANCE SPECTRE

*Screenplay by Donald James*
*Directed by Peter Medak*
*With Ken Hutchinson as Sanderson*

The planet Tora is sighted, but it is on a collision course with the Moon. When Koenig orders that the Command Centre be made off-limits, a small group of Alphans are angered. Under the leadership of Sanderson, they use their laser guns to take over the Command Centre. Then they hold a seance, and claim that they can 'see' that Tora would be habitable. Koenig quickly regains control, and though the rebels are

confined for medical tests, they escape. Koenig is now faced, with two problems - the imminent collision with Tora, and Sanderson, who could upset all their chances

## 21. DORZAC

*Screenplay by Christopher Penfold*
*Directed by Val Guest*
*With Lee Montague as Dorzac*
*Jill Townsend as Sahala*

A fantastic spaceship arrives and is given permission to land on the Moon. A beautiful young woman named Sahala emerges from it, seeking medical attention for a crew member who she says was injured by a dangerous criminal they have captured. But when the criminal turns out to be a man from Maya's home planet, Psychon, named Dorzac, and he persuades Maya that he was not responsible for evil acts Sahala accused him of, the trouble begins.

## 22. DEVIL'S PLANET

*Screenplay by Michael Winder*
*Directed by Tom Clegg*
*With Hildegard Neil as Elizia*
*Michael Dickinson as Maine*

Answering a distress signal, Koenig and Blake Maine go first to the desolate planet Ellna, and then to its moon, Entra, where their Eagle goes out of control and crash lands. The first thing they see is a man being chased by three beautiful girls dressed in skin-tight catsuits and carrying long, electric whips! It turns out that Entra is Ellna's penal colony; within minutes Maine is killed, and then Koenig is imprisoned. Can he escape or be rescued by Alphans?

## 23. THE IMMUNITY SYNDROME

*Screenplay by Johnny Byrne*
*Directed by Bob Brooks*
*With Nadim Sawalha as Zoran*

On a seemingly inhabitable planet, a series of misfortunes befall Alpha's advance party. Tony Verdeschi is rendered insane by a piercing sound coupled with a blinding light. The metal in their Eagle violently corrodes and the craft starts to fall apart. Two Alphans die after drinking spring water that had been tested and found pure. Then, inside a strange, geodetic structure, they find the skeleton of a uniformed man. But before he died, the man, named Zoran, made a video recording explaining how any future visitors to the planet might survive.

## 24. THE DORCONS

*Screenplay by Johnny Byrne*
*Directed by Tom Clegg*
*With Patrick Troughton as Archon*
*Ann Firbank as Varda*
*Gerry Sundquist as Malic*

Maya is terrified when a huge alien spaceship materialises nearby, as she recognises it as a Dorcon ship - the Dorcons being the most powerful race in the galaxy. She explains that Dorcons have hounded Psychons for centuries, believing that the brain stem from a Psychon can give them immortality. When the three Dorcon leaders, the Supreme Archon, Consul Varda and Archon's nephew Malic, demand Maya be sent to them, Koenig refuses. So Varda comes aboard Alpha and Maya is taken by force. But Koenig manages to go with her to the Dorcon ship, and using the power struggle between the three Dorcon leaders, creates an opportunity for Maya to be rescued.

### Principal credits (series 1)

24 sixty minute episodes
An ITC/RAI Co-Production
Produced by Group Three for
ITC World-Wide Distribution
Executive Producer: Gerry Anderson
Producer: Sylvia Anderson
Series created by
Gerry and Sylvia Anderson

Story Consultant: Christopher Penfold
Script Editors: Johnny Byrne/
Edward Di Lorenzo
Music by : Barry Gray
Special Effects: Brian Johnson
Moon City Costumes designed by :
Rudi Gernreich
Art Director: Keith Wilson

### Additional Credits (series II)

24 sixty minute episodes
A Gerry Anderson Production for ITC
Entertainment
Created by Gerry and Sylvia Anderson
Executive Producer: Gerry Anderson
Producer and Story Editor: Fred
Freiberger

1983

In the year 2020 alien spaceships approach the planet Mars. The NASA Expedition HQ is spectacularly destroyed. The androids have journeyed from the planet Guk and their witch-like commander Zelda sets up her base on Mars and plans the destruction of human beings on Earth. Alerted by the 1st Alien Attack in 2017, the UN High Command appoints Dr Tiger Ninestein to set up an elite international fighting force to defend the world. This small dedicated team is called the Terrahawks. From their secret base somewhere in South America they develop their sophisticated weaponry for the fight to come.

## THE TERRAHAWKS

**DR TIGER NINESTEIN -**
One of nine clones of the brilliant Professor Stein. After a distinguished military career, he was persuaded to mastermind the creation of, and to become the first commander of, the TERRAHAWKS Earth Defence Squadron.

**CAPTAIN MARY FALCONER -**
previously a civilian pilot and free-fall parachutist before gaining space mission experience and being selected for TERRAHAWKS assignments. Cool, charming and efficient, she pilots the TERRAHAWKS spacecraft, Battlehawk.

**LIEUTENANT HIRO -**
selected by Dr Ninestein for TERRAHAWKS because of his phenomenal intelligence and advanced research into high technology projects. He designed the TERRAHAWKS Computer Command Centre.

**CAPTAIN KATE KESTREL -**
an extrovert member of the team, seconded to TERRAHAWKS as a Hawkwing pilot 2018, following extensive space mission experience but also an internationally known singing star.

**LIEUTENANT HAWKEYE -**
an excellent pilot, whose micro-computer assisted eyes give him lightning reflexes in flying and high speed gunnery.

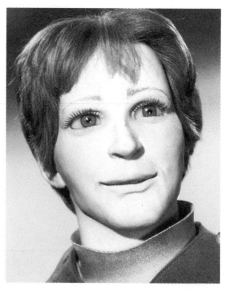

**SERGEANT MAJOR ZERO -**
Zeroid commander on Earth. His power source induces 'emotions' normally associated with humans.

**SPACE SERGEANT 101 -**
a specially modified zeroid programmed to exercise supervisory and organisational tasks in space away from human direction.

## THE ALIENS

**ZELDA, IMPERIAL QUEEN OF THE PLANET GUK -**
an android, accidentally given the power of self-determination. Her main aim is the galactic domination and enslavement of humanoids. She combines the age and 'beauty' of a humanoid with the mysterious powers and energy of a machine.

**CYSTAR -**
sister of Zelda and created by her. Bubbly but feather-brained, her inferior brain circuitry ensures her domination by Zelda.

**YUNGSTAR -**
son of Zelda and created by her. Cowardly, lazy, spoiled and greedy, he has a penchant for carbon jelly and granite crunchies.

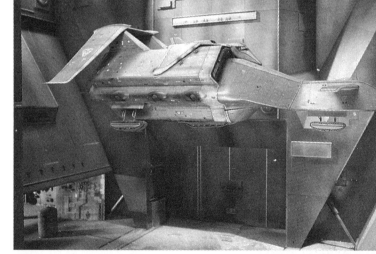

## 1. EXPECT THE UNEXPECTED (Part 1)
*Written by Gerry Anderson*

The year is 2020. Mars has been invaded by the evil android Zelda. On Earth, an elite fighting force - the Terrahawks - stand ready at their secret base to counter Zelda's first attack.

## 2. EXPECT THE UNEXPECTED (Part 2)
*Written by Gerry Anderson*
*Directed by Alan Pattillo*

Zelda launches her second attack. Using her incredible powers and aided by her robot cubes she traps Ninestein and Mary in a force field. Fortunately, Zero comes to the rescue in time.

## 3. THUNDER ROAR
*Written by Tony Barwick*
*Directed by Alan Pattillo*

Zelda releases a hideous space monster, Sram, from cryogenic sleep. His task is to destroy the Terrahawks with the aid of his thunderous voice which can destroy mountains

## 4. CLOSE CALL
*Written by Tony Barwick*
*Directed by Desmond Saunders*

The Overlander, a gigantic futuristic land train, is driving across country with vital supplies for Hawknest. Darrel, a reporter under Zelda's control, hijacks the transporter.

## 5. FROM HERE TO ETERNITY
*Written by Tony Barwick*
*Directed by Alan Pattillo*

Spacehawk sights the battered remains of Space Probe Alpha, which was never designed to return to Earth. The Terrahawks investigate and find a gravity bomb aboard intended for Hawknest.

## 6. SPACE SAMURAI
*Written by Tony Barwick*
*Directed by Desmond Saunders*

Tamura, a Space Samurai, and commander of a powerful space cruiser insists that Zelda and Ninestein meet to resolve their differences.

## 7. THE SPORILLA
*Written by Tony Barwick*
*Directed by Tony Bell*

The Terrahawks travel to the distant moon Calisto. An unmanned remote tracker station on the surface has gone off the air. When they arrive, they are faced by the Sporilla, one of Zelda's monsters.

## 8. HAPPY MADEDAY
*Written by Tony Barwick*
*Directed by Tony Lenny*

Moid, master of infinite disguise, travels to Earth. Hiro is forced to crash and Moid, disguised as Spacehawk's commander, takes his place. Zelda then launches a massive attack.

## 9. GUNFIGHT AT OAKY'S CORRAL
*Written by Tony Barwick*
*Directed by Tony Bell*

After a gunfight between Zelda's cubes and Sergeant Major Zero in the Arizona desert, one cube escapes. Ninestein leads the chase and finds himself in a final shoot out.

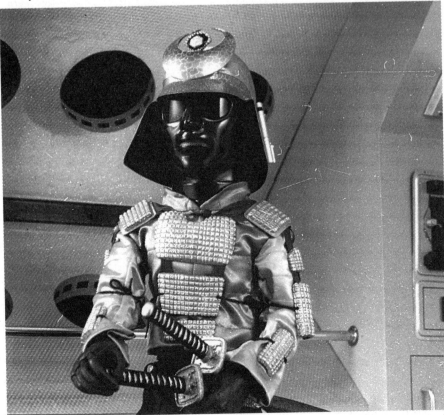

## 10. THE UGLIEST MONSTER OF ALL

*Written by Tony Barwick*
*Directed by Tony Lenny*

Zelda releases the ugliest monster of all from cryogenic storage. It is a cuddly space bear called Yuri which the Terrahawks take to their hearts not realising its strange and terrible powers.

## 11. THE GUN

*Written by Tony Barwick*
*Directed by Tony Bell*

An unmanned space transporter returns to Earth carrying rare tungsten ore. It is a quarter of a million miles off course. The Terrahawks shoot it down but Zelda has other plans.

## 12. THUNDER PATH

*Written by Tony Barwick*
*Directed by Tony Lenny*

The Overlander, the giant land train that brings supplies to the Terrahawks' secret base, is hijacked by Sram. The monster drives straight towards an oil refinery and must be stopped.

## 13. MIND MONSTER

*Written by Tony Barwick*
*Directed by Tony Bell*

The Terrahawks discover a space capsule and take it to Spacehawk. Although the capsule looks empty, it contains a mind monster capable of producing amazing hallucinations.

## 14. TO CATCH A TIGER

*Written by Tony Barwick*
*Directed by Tony Lenny*

Zelda captures the two-man crew of a space transporter. They are held hostage and Zelda will only release them in exchange for Ninestein. The Terrahawks leader must face his enemy on her own territory.

## 15. THE MIDAS TOUCH

*Written by Trevor Lansdown and Tony Barwick*
*Directed by Alan Pattillo*

The world's gold reserves are locked in a space Fort Knox. Zelda realises that the destruction of this space ship would cause economic havoc. She sends Krell to Earth where the Terrahawks must destroy it.

## 16. OPERATION SAS

*Written by Tony Barwick*
*Directed by Tony Lenny*

Kate is held captive by Yungstar and Yuri the Space Bear. The rescue mission is in the 'hands' of Zero and his zeroids, SAS style.

## 17. TEN TOP POP

*Written by Tony Barwick*
*Directed by Tony Bell*

Yungstar listens to pop music from Earth on his 'Ferret' but Zelda decides to transmit back. She takes control of Stew Dapples, the A & R man at Anderburr Records, to aid her in the next attack on Earth.

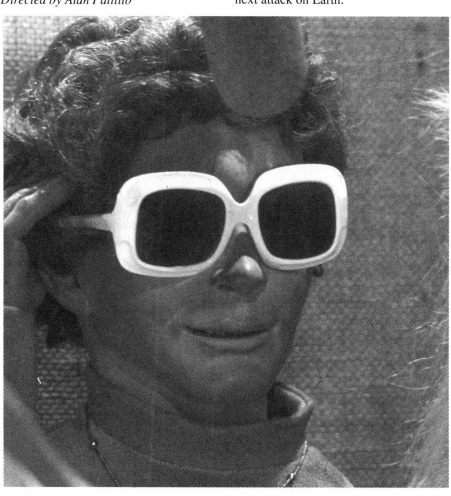

## 18. UNSEEN MENACE
*Written by Tony Barwick*
*Directed by Tony Bell*

Moid, Master of Infinite Disguise, has perfected his most awesome impersonation. He travels to Earth disguised as the Invisible Man to create havoc among the Terrahawks.

## 19. A CHRISTMAS MIRACLE
*Written by Tony Barwick*
*Directed by Tony Lenny*

It is Christmas Eve and all at Hawknest prepare to celebrate. Zelda, however, realising their guard will be down, launches an all-out attack.

## 20. MIDNIGHT BLUE
*Written by Tony Barwick*
*Directed by Tony Lenny*

Spacehawk fires at a Zeaf but it gets through. Hawkwing takes up the chase. Ninestein realises that the Zeaf is miniaturised but it is too late and the Hawkwing is trapped in space.

## 21. PLAY IT AGAIN, SRAM
*Written by Tony Barwick*
*Directed by Tony Bell*

Kate Kestrel wins the World Song Contest. However, Zelda throws out a challenge saying that she too has a song. An Interstellar Song Contest is arranged but Sram is lurking to destroy the Terrahawks.

## 22. MY KINGDOM FOR A ZEAF
*Written by Tony Barwick*
*Directed by Tony Bell*

Zelda unleashes a new menace against the Terrahawks. Lord Tempo, Master of Time, can travel back and forth in time and space and comes to Earth with Yungstar. Kate Kestrel is their target.

## 23. ZERO'S FINEST HOUR
*Written by Tony Barwick*
*Directed by Tony Bell*

Yungstar attempts to follow the Overlander to Hawknest. With Ninestein and the rest of the Terrahawks out of action, Zero and his men must handle the situation.

## 24. THE ULTIMATE MENACE
*Written by Tony Barwick*
*Directed by Tony Lenny*

Zelda and Ninestein are forced to join forces against the ultimate machine, a powerful space ship controlled by a massive computer. It seems unstoppable but Sergeant Major Zero saves the day.

## 25. GOLD
*Written by Tony Barwick*
*Directed by Desmond Saunders*

While the zeroids explore the crater on a meteorite they think they have found a huge nugget of gold. Secretly they bring it back to Hawknest, but it is a golden bomb planted by Zelda.

## 26. MA'S MONSTERS
*Written by Tony Barwick*
*Directed by Tony Bell*

Zelda recalls the exploits of her Monsters. Many have fought the Terrahawks but all have failed. Zelda has a surprise, a new cryogenic store of monsters. And Cystar reveals she is going to have a baby!

## 27. TWO FOR THE PRICE OF ONE
*Written by Tony Barwick*
*Directed by Tony Lenny*

The Terrahawks plan a surprise attack on Zelda's complex on Mars. The opposition seems preoccupied and as the Terrahawks close in they learn why. Cystar has decided to have a baby. . .

## 28. CHILD'S PLAY
*Written by Tony Barwick*
*Directed by Tony Bell*

Birlgoy - the baby Cystar built - devises a cunning plan. The Terrahawks discover a large explosive device, but why has it been planted out in the desert? As Mary goes to diffuse it, the fiendish trap is sprung.

## 29. JOLLY ROGER ONE

*Written by Tony Barwick*
*Directed by Tony Lenny*

Captain Goat flies his space galleon with Yungstar and Birlgoy aboard to face the accursed Terrahawks. It will be a space ship shoot-out as in the days of pirates and walking the plank.

## 30. RUNAWAY

*Written by Tony Barwick*
*Directed by Tony Bell*

Why has Zelda allowed Yungstar to run away to Earth ? He will be captured. What the Terrahawks do not realise is that Yungstar has been bugged by the devious Birlgoy. Will Zelda finally discover the location of Hawknest ?

## 31. FIRST STRIKE

*Written by Tony Barwick*
*Directed by Tony Lenny*

General Cord has been given the Authority to lead a first strike against Zelda. Ninestein warns him that it won't work, but the General refuses to listen. Zelda mobilises Lord Tempo and Yuri the Space Bear.

## 32. TERRABOMB

*Written by Tony Barwick*
*Directed by Tony Lenny*

The Battletank checks out a Zeaf but it vanishes as Zelda reclaims her own. The Terrahawks return to base only to discover they have brought an alien space bomb back to Hawknest.

## 33. DOPPELGANGER

*Written by Tony Barwick*
*Directed by Tony Lenny*

Birlgoy has found a way of making an exact replica of Yungstar. This statue appears in a museum. The Terrahawks are mystified - why is Zelda producing Doppelgangers ? Then, we see the statue move . . .

## 34. TIMEWARP

*Written by Tony Barwick*
*Directed by Tony Bell*

Spacehawk destroyed . . . Hawknest under attack . . . what is happening ? It's all in Mary's imagination but it was all so real. Lord Tempo is trying to induce a timewarp into the Terrahawks organisation - and he will try again.

## 35. SPACE CYCLOPS

*Written by Tony Barwick*
*Directed by Tony Lenny*

On the lunar surface, a strange monster feeds on the wreckage of a space module. Zelda watches in delight as the Cyclops grows in size and power. How will the Terrahawks stop this metal eating maniac ?

## 36. OPERATION ZERO

*Written by Tony Barwick*
*Directed by Tony Lenny*

Sergeant Major Zero isn't feeling too good - but the news is worse. Three aliens are on the loose in Hawknest. The situation becomes desperate - the whole base is about to be destroyed. It's a frightening nightmare.

## 37. SPACE GIANT

*Written by Tony Barwick*
*Directed by Tony Lenny*

When two Space Miners capture a small Sporilla they decide to smuggle it back to Earth. But it is all part of Zelda's evil plan. A terrifying monster is unleashed.

## 38. CRY UFO

*Written by Tony Barwick*
*Directed by Tony Bell*

Everything is going wrong for Stew Dapples and when he sees a UFO no-one believes him. But the UFO is part of Zelda's plan - the Terrahawks must seek and destroy it.

## 39. COLD FINGER

*Written by Tony Barwick*
*Directed by Tony Bell*

Zelda goes to meet Cold Finger. Everything in his space ship is made of ice. They plan to attack Earth, bombard it with millions of tons of ice. Terrahawks must counter the threat.

**Voices**
Windsor Davies
Denise Bryer
Jeremy Hitcher
Anne Ridler
Ben Stevens

**Principal credits**
39 thirty minute episodes
Colour
An Anderson Burr Pictures / LWT Production
Created by Gerry Anderson
Produced by Gerry Anderson and Christopher Burr
Music by Richard Harvey
Additional music by Gerry Anderson and Christopher Burr
Special effects by Stephen Begg

1987

Dick Spanner is a private investigator in the classic tradition: a wise-cracking down-at-heel detective in a trench coat and fedora.His cases, which occur not so long ago, in a parallel universe not far from here, take him down many dark, mean streets.He is threatened by thugs, wrongly imprisoned by the police , fed spiked drinks in sleazy clubs and has mysterious dealings with glamorous women. With a pun for every occasion, he manages to come through unscathed and solve the crime.

## Characters

DICK SPANNER-
robot private detective. A Humphrey Bogart type, with a cool line in dialogue.

MAE EAST -
glamorous blonde bombshell, with more curves than a mountain railway!

LIEUTENANT O'GRADY -
bull-necked, suspicious policeman, keen to see Dick behind bars.

## 1. THE CASE OF THE HUMAN CANNON BALL

*Written by Harry Bolt*
*Directed by Terry Adlam*

Harry the Human Cannon Ball has gone missing and Dick Spanner, Private Investigator, sets out to track him down. Along the way the persistent Lieutenant O'Grady tries to throw him in jail, 'The Fatman', Sidney Sidestreet, gives him advice and the villainous goons of Mendoza try to kill him. The link between the Human Cannon Ball's disappearance and the number of flying Mexicans in town lead Dick to the world of the circus and he has to untangle an evil scheme masterminded by 'The Fatman'.

## 2. THE CASE OF THE MALTESE PARROT

*Written by Harry Bolt*
*Directed by Terry Adlam*

The disappearance of the famous Maltese parrot takes Dick Spanner, Private Investigator on the trail to Ivywood, movie capital of the world. There the plot gets murkier; he meets silent film star, Gloria Vamp, heavies George Lifeboat and Edward G. Hobson, sexpot Mae East and director Eric von Strongbow. He is double-crossed, tied to a railway track, attacked by a giant tin opener and much more before he solves the mystery of the parrot's disappearance and its link with the invasion of Ivywood by 'smalls' .

### Principal credits

2 fifty-five minute stories
Colour
Made by the Anderson Burr Partnership in association with Channel 4
Produced by: Gerry Anderson and Christopher Burr
Based on an original idea by: Terry Adlam
Creative supervision by: Gerry Anderson
Production Coordinator: Mary Anderson
Music composed and performed by: Christopher Burr
Voice of Dick Spanner: Shane Rimmer

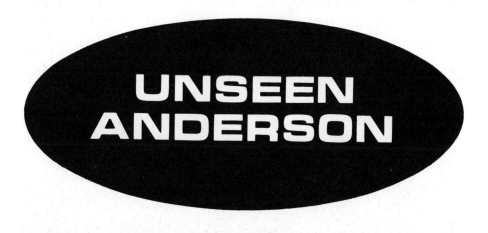

The following is a brief outline of Gerry Anderson projects for television which did not get beyond the proposal or pilot episode stage: Rescue 4 reached outline stage and was a proposed live action series for the US network NBC. The Investigator was a pilot episode also prepared for NBC, featuring live action, puppets and models. Space Police was a science fiction pilot episode prepared by Anderson Burr, featuring live action and puppets.

## INTER-GALACTIC RESCUE: RESCUE 4
### Premise

A multi-purpose craft has a four-man crew. It has vertical take-off and landing ability. It is sea-going and can submerge. By lowering a skirt and using thruster motors, the craft is a hovercraft.

### Principal credits
Series created by Gerry Anderson and Fred Freiberger.
Vehicle design by Gerry Anderson, Reg Hill and Brian Johnson. Model craft made by Martin Bower.

## THE INVESTIGATOR
### Premise

The Investigator, a being from another galaxy, chooses a boy and girl, John and Julie, to help him to right wrongs on Earth. John and Julie are 'miniaturised' to help them in their missions, and have a specially adapted car with listening devices and scanners.

### 1. THE INVESTIGATOR
Julie and John are contacted on Malta by 'THe Investigator'. He wants them to prevnt the theft of a priceless painting by the wealty Stavros Karanti. Julie and John follow Karanti and his accomplice Christoph to the church where the painting is kept. Through deceit, Karanti and Christoph steal the painting and escape with John and Julie in pursuit.Karanti takes off in his private plane but is forced to confess and turn himself in to the authorities by John, who concealed on the plane in miniature form, appears to Karanti to be the voice of his conscience.

### Principal credits
Devised and directed by: Gerry Anderson
Story by: Shane Rimmer
Screenplay by: Sylvia Anderson
Models by: Reg Hill
Artists:
Karanti - Charles Thake
Christoph - Peter Borg
Voice Artists:
Julie - Sylvia Anderson
John - Shane Rimmer
The Investigator - Peter Dyneley

## SPACE POLICE
### Premise

Lt Brogan is the grizzled, old-fashioned commanding officer of Space Police: Precinct 44 and the pilot episode 'Star Laws' involves his continuing battle against the forces of organised crime, led by V. Lann.

### Characters
LIEUTENANT BROGAN - commanding officer of Space Police: Precinct 44
CATHY COSTELLO -officer in the Space Police
BATS - a cat-like female officer with amazing sensory powers
SLOMO - the quirky police computer
V. LANN - head of organised crime in Precinct 44
E. VILE - V. Lann's side-kick
MEGABITE - V. Lann's fierce metallic guard dog
TOM,DICK and HARRY - alien members of Space Police

### 1. STAR LAWS
Lt Brogan warns the planet's President of the possible dangers from V. Lann and his hoods. The President, undeterred, decides to travel to Ultraville by monorail. However, Bron, the President's aide, has given the security code for the monorail to V. Lann in exchange for his family's safety. The monorail is booby trapped and V. Lann delivers an ultimatum: the release of his men or the President dies. Bats, a Space Police officer on the train, discovers the bomb and defuses it. V Lann has another go; he destroys a rail bridge ahead of the monorail. The engine accelerates and only in the nick of time is the engine exploded and the train halted at the edge of the shattered bridge.

An Anderson Burr Picture
Series created and produced by: Gerry Anderson and Christopher Burr
Written by: Gerry Anderson and Tony Barwick
Directed by: Tony Bell
Music by: Christopher Burr and Gerry Anderson
Visual effects by: Stephen Begg

## Colour photographic section - key

1. *SUPERCAR* - Mike Mercury, Mitch and Dr Beaker
2. *SUPERCAR* - Mike Mercury in Supercar
3. *FIREBALL XL5* - Robert the Robot, Venus and Steve Zodiac
   in Fireball XL5
4. *FIREBALL XL5* - Fireball XL5 blasts off into space
5. *STINGRAY* - Troy Tempest, Marina and 'Phones'
6. *STINGRAY* - Stingray pursued by one of Titan's Terror Fish

7. *THUNDERBIRDS* - Thunderbird 1 in pursuit
8. *THUNDERBIRDS* - John Tracy in Thunderbird 5
9. *THUNDERBIRDS* - Thunderbird 4 underwater
10. *THUNDERBIRDS* - Brains, Virgil and Gordon in
    Thunderbird 2
11. *THUNDERBIRDS* - Parker in trouble
12. *THUNDERBIRDS* - the swimming pool on Tracy Island
13. *THUNDERBIRDS* - the villainous Hood
14. *THUNDERBIRDS* - Thunderbird 2 to the rescue

15. *CAPTAIN SCARLET* - The Spectrum Pursuit Vehicle with
    three Angels overhead
16. *CAPTAIN SCARLET* - an Angel aircraft
17. *CAPTAIN SCARLET* - Colonel White briefs Captain Scarlet,
    Captain Blue and Lieutenant Green
18. *CAPTAIN SCARLET* - the Angels in the 'Orange Room'
19. *CAPTAIN SCARLET* - Cloudbase, Spectrum HQ,
    under attack
20. *CAPTAIN SCARLET* - Captain Black, agent of
    the Mysterons
21. *CAPTAIN SCARLET* - the Spectrum Saloon Car
22. *CAPTAIN SCARLET* - the indestructible Captain Scarlet
23. *CAPTAIN SCARLET* - Lieutenant Green at the controls

24. *JOE 90* - Joe 90 in BIG RAT
25. *JOE 90* - Joe 90, 'Mac' and Sam Loover
26. *JOE 90* - Mac's car
27. *JOE 90* - Joe 90's WIN badge
28. *THE SECRET SERVICE* - Father Unwin in his car, Gabriel
29. *THE SECRET SERVICE* - the 'minimiser' concealed
    in a book

30. *THE PROTECTORS* - the Contessa and Harry Rule
31. *UFO* - Lieutenant Gay Ellis
32. *UFO* - Straker and Foreman witness an autopsy
33. *UFO* - Lunar module with satellite in orbit
34. *SPACE 1999* - An Eagle passes over the lunar surface
35. *SPACE 1999* - Koenig and Russell lead an exploratory party

36. *TERRAHAWKS* - Sergeant Major Zero
37. *TERRAHAWKS* - Zelda, Cystar, Yungstar, Sporilla and Sram
38. *TERRAHAWKS* - Hawknest, Terrahawks' HQ
39. *DICK SPANNER* - Dick Spanner, Private Investigator
40. *DICK SPANNER* - Mae East, blonde bombshell
41. *SPACE POLICE* - 'Dick' and 'Harry' tackle an alien

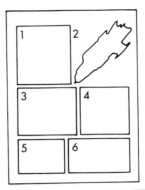
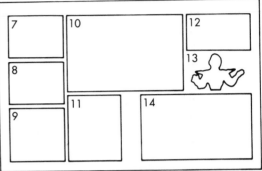
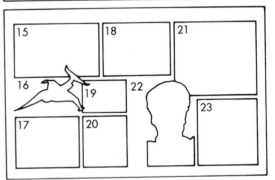
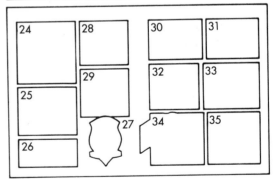
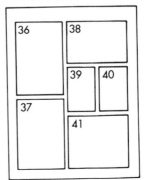

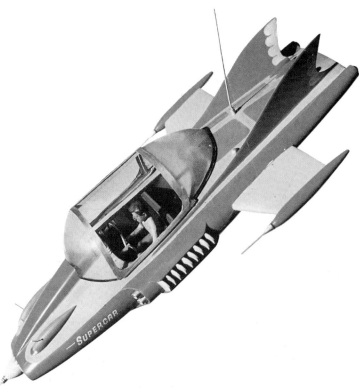